The
Sucaryl®
BRAND
Cookbook of
SUGAR-FREE RECIPES

The Sucaryl®

BRAND

Cookbook of

SUGAR-FREE RECIPES

by Sara Hervey Watts

Random House • New York

All recipes in *The Sucaryl Cookbook of Sugar-free Recipes* were tested and developed with *Sucaryl* brand liquid sweetener.

All recipes have been tested by Betty Barlow, a graduate home economist. The food exchanges in this book have been calculated by Emma Seifrit Weigley, a graduate home economist and dietitian.

Before making any substitutions in a diabetic diet, consult your physician.

Second Printing

Copyright© 1968 by Random House, Inc.

All rights reserved under International and Pan-American Copyright Conventions. Published in the United States by Random House, Inc., New York, and simultaneously in Canada by Random House of Canada Limited, Toronto.

Library of Congress Catalog Card Number: 68-28540

Manufactured in the United States of America
Spot illustrations by William Lahey Cummings

Contents

The Sucaryl® BRAND

Cookbook of

SUGAR-FREE RECIPES

SWEET TALK

This comprehensive collection of deliciously sweet yet *sugar-free* recipes has been designed for those who long for the sweet things of life . . . without the penalties of sugar's calories. Almost everyone who loves to eat loves sweets. Half a grapefruit at the end of a meal, although satisfactory on occasion, will not satisfy the craving for something tantalizingly sweet and rich-tasting. Nor is "just a taste" the answer.

Many weight watchers, as soon as they notice the pointer on the bathroom scale moving onward and upward, woefully decide that desserts must go. Happily, such self-denial is not always warranted. Although almost all heavyweights get that way partly because they have a sweet tooth, sweets are important to the dieter's morale. When desserts have been an anticipated part of the day's menu, weight watchers feel cheated if they no longer can end the meal with a sweet treat.

Calorie-concerned cooks now know that there is a solution to the age-old problem of having your cake and eating it too. By simply substituting low-calorie, even no-calorie, ingredients for those with an excessively high calorie tab, worthwhile calorie reductions can be accomplished in many calorie-laden dishes . . . without changing the recipe's basic appetite appeal or good taste.

Often it's the little things in cooking that make the big calorie difference, a little thing like sugar, for instance. Each cup of sugar in a recipe adds 864 extra calories, calories that dieters neither want nor need if they're seriously trying to lose weight. Fortunately, thanks to man's inventiveness, low-calorie sweeteners have been developed which taste just as satisfyingly sweet as sugar. Among these sweeteners, *Sucaryl** (brand sweeteners) is one favored by cooks because of its flavor and because of its stability to heat and cold. This is a sweetener you really can cook with. Even at high cooking temperatures (and freezer temperatures), it doesn't turn bitter nor lose its sugar-sweet taste.

With the help of *Sucaryl* sweeteners, dieters no longer need resist the temptation of blissfully sweet desserts and other delectable dishes normally requiring sugar. When you use *Sucaryl* to replace sugar, you eliminate all the extra, unnecessary calories of sugar, yet pleasurable sweetness and appetite appeal remain unchanged.

All of the recipes in *The Sucaryl Cookbook of Sugar-free Recipes* are calorie-trimmed, sugar-free adaptations of traditional favorites. Calories in these recipes have been trimmed to a fraction of their usual counts. The sweet result is that you can enjoy a respectable portion, large enough to be satisfying, without risk of overindulgence.

Calorie savings in the recipes are dramatic. In most of the desserts, as well as in other sweetened foods, you save from one-third to two-thirds of the total calories simply by using a *Sucaryl* sweetener. Note that calories per serving are given with

Sucaryl is the trademark of Abbott Laboratories for its line of low-calorie and noncalorie sweeteners.

each recipe; in addition there is a nutritional analysis of the protein, fat and carbohydrate content. For the convenience of those on a food exchange diet, exchanges have also been included. And so that you may quickly compute the calories you save, calorie counts for the recipes when sweetened with sugar are also given.

Special Note to Diabetics:

No refined sugar, as such, has been added to any of the recipes in *The Sucaryl Cookbook of Sugar-Free Recipes*. Remember, however, that fruits and vegetables contain natural sugars, and that certain prepared food products may contain refined sugar. (For example, dried shredded coconut, cereals, graham crackers, lady fingers, maraschino cherries, semi-sweet chocolate pieces, Tabasco, soy sauce, Worcestershire sauce.) If in doubt about a recipe containing any one of these ingredients, consult your physician before including it in your diet. Recipes containing alcohol are not usually permitted in a diabetic diet (unless the amount per serving is negligible). *Before making any substitutions in a diabetic diet, consult your physician.*

SWEET FACTS AND FIGURES

As a nation, we're badly out of shape. It's reported that at least 30 percent of the male population and 40 percent of the females over the age of forty years are more than 20 percent above their best weight. It appears, however, that we're doing something about it.

In recent years our figure-fretting public has become increasingly aware of the importance of weight control. An unprecedented barrage of warnings about obesity has been aimed at our overweight populace. As medical science has shown excessive weight to be a causative factor in high mortality, Americans have become more conscious of the need to discipline their diets.

As a result, success in losing excess poundage is becoming more and more evident. Women weigh about five pounds less than those of the same height in 1912. Twenty-five years ago the smallest size stocked by the average dress shop was twelve or fourteen. Today, size-six and -eight dresses are stocked, and sold.

Bizarre "wonder diets" are losing ground. After the rash of off-again, on-again crash diets of the fifties, it's a relief to discover that most weight-reduction plans today (at least those most generally favored by doctors and nutritionists) recommend that normal diet patterns be followed as closely as possible, but that effort be made to avoid excess "empty" calories.

As a prudent weight watcher, you need to concern yourself not only with the *number* of calories you eat, but with the *quality* of those calories. It makes good diet sense to choose your calories from foods that pay nutritional "dividends" so that strength, good health and a sense of well-being can be maintained. Learn which foods are basic and which are literally "frosting," if you are to cut down weight safely. Cutting down on calories, but keeping a sensible balance of all the protective foods, is recognized as the logical way to become and stay slim.

Teen-age overweight is one of our most serious nutritional problems. It has been well documented that 20 to 30 percent of the teen-age population is "significantly overweight"; that 15 to 20 percent can be classed as "genuine medical problems." Chances are that the fat child will turn into the fat grownup, unless calories are curbed and poor eating habits corrected at an early age.

Two reasons have been suggested as to why there are so many overweight children today. These are lack of physical exercise, coupled with an excess of sweets. The Council on Foods and Nutrition of the American Medical Association put it this way: "Common concentrated sweets used to excess are harmful especially for children, insofar as they impair the appetite for other highly necessary foods and lead to reduced intake of milk, eggs, fruits, vegetables, meat and cereals."

Be smart about calories. Everyone knows, or should know by now, that calories DO count. They add, they multiply, but unfortunately they never subtract. Those who are talented in culinary arithmetic change pluses into minuses by eliminating calories before they get a chance to play havoc with hips and waistlines and chins.

The word "calorie" has become a commonplace household term, yet many people don't know its real meaning. The much talked-of calorie is merely a convenient unit for the measurement of energy. It is not food nor heat as such, but a measure of the amount of energy produced by different foods by their combustion in the body. If you want to be technical, one calorie represents the amount of heat required to raise the temperature of one pound of water 4° Fahrenheit. Obviously, if we consume more calories than the body "burns up" or oxidizes, we gain weight. Conversely, if our calorie intake is less than our energy needs, stored body fat is burned and we lose weight.

It isn't enough, however, to know the definition of a calorie, or even the number of calories in various foods. We should also know how many calories we personally need to keep trim and full of health.

Figure your individual calorie needs. For a general approximation of your own calorie requirements, first decide on your "ideal" weight. (Height-weight-age charts may be used as a guide.) Then multiply this ideal weight by 15 if you are moderately active (housewives and office workers are in this group); by 18 to 20 if you are more active. (Example: 130 pounds (ideal weight) × 15 calories = 1950 calories.) This is your average daily calorie maintenance level.

In order to lose one pound of body fat, you must eat 3500 fewer calories than your maintenance level. Thus, if you consume 500 fewer calories each day of seven days, you should lose weight at the rate of one pound per week. If you need to lose pounds to achieve your ideal weight, subtract 500 calories from your maintenance level. (1950 calories − 500 calories = 1450 calories.) This, then, is your daily calorie limit while on your weight-reduction program.

Hold that line. Once you have achieved your desired weight, you'll want to keep it. At this point, you may *gradually* increase your calorie intake up to, but not beyond, your established maintenance level. Remember, just 100 extra calories a day over a period of a year (36,500 calories) add up to ten unwanted pounds; in two years, twenty pounds . . . and next thing you know, middle-age spread!

Beware of creeping pounds. It's sad, but it's true . . . after the age of thirty we need to begin eating a little less in order to weigh the same. As we grow older, cell activity throughout the body declines and we need fewer calories to maintain body weight. If we don't gradually reduce our food intake, there will be a gradual increase in weight, which in the course of fifteen or twenty years can become appreciable.

So keep an eye on the scales. If you gain three pounds over ideal weight, get rid of them right away. It's much easier, less discouraging, too, than to pile up a lot of excess poundage and then try to take it off. If you never gain five extra pounds, you'll never gain ten. And of course, if you never gain ten, you'll never have a serious weight problem.

Even small calorie savings can be worthwhile. Just how effective can dietary sweeteners be in controlling weight? Some people recently have suggested that it's "wishful thinking" to suppose that you can get any benefit from the use of low-calorie sweeteners. The implication is that the *numbers* of calories saved are not adequate to produce a weight difference.

When you talk about a low-calorie sweetener such as *Sucaryl,* you're talking generally in the range of from 100 to 300 calories saved a day. Pretty modest next to the crash programs. Is this enough to do any good?

As we have pointed out, a simple reduction of no more than 100 calories a day could make the difference between overweight and ideal weight for millions of Americans. Many overweights become that way because they *regularly eat a little more than they should*, rather than because they stuff themselves. It's encouraging to realize that you can drop nearly a pound of fat in a month's time, simply by subtracting a mere 100 calories a day from your diet. (Obviously, if you've been gaining more than a pound a month, you'll want to double or triple your daily calorie cutback.) With the help of *Sucaryl* sweeteners, it's easy to slash away 100 calories or more each day . . . and without the hardship of giving up favorite foods or beverages.

Calories saved by sweetening coffee and tea the sugar-free way should not be dismissed lightly. Just how worthwhile are these calorie savings? Let's do some figuring. One level teaspoon of sugar contains 18 calories. If you were to drink only three cups of coffee a day, and if you sweetened each cup with the *Sucaryl* sweetener equivalent of from one to two level teaspoons of sugar, it's apparent that you'd save from 54 to 108 calories by this simple expedient alone. In a year's time the calorie savings would total approximately 20,000 to 40,000 calories, a theoretical equivalent of from five to ten pounds of body fat. There is no such thing as an "insignificant" calorie.

SPECIAL FACTS
ABOUT *SUCARYL*

Liquid *Sucaryl* is a cyclamate-type sweetener, ideal for cookery as well as for sweetening both cold and hot beverages. It's easy to measure, it disperses instantly and evenly and it retains its natural-tasting sweetness at both high cooking temperatures and freezing temperatures. Functional *Sucaryl* table bottles come in 6-, 12- and 20-fluid-ounce sizes. (Also available: a pocket-size "squeeze" bottle.) Liquid *Sucaryl* is produced in two formulations, *Sucaryl* brand sodium sweetener and *Sucaryl* brand calcium sweetener. The calcium form contains no sodium, and therefore is suitable for persons on low-sodium diets.

***Sucaryl* in tablet form** is popular for sweetening hot drinks. If used in cooking, dissolve the tablets in a small amount of hot water equivalent to the amount of liquid *Sucaryl* called for in the recipe. (See "*Sucaryl*-Sugar Equivalencies," page 235.) Bottles of 100, 250 and 1000 tablets are available, as well as a refillable pocket dispenser. Both calcium cyclamate and sodium cyclamate tablets are produced.

Grànulated *Sucaryl* is another popular form of dietary sweetener, useful for sprinkling on fruits, cereal and other foods. Available in the calcium cyclamate form, and packaged in a 1½-ounce shaker-top glass bottle with a measuring cap, this sweetener looks like sugar, sprinkles like sugar and sweetens with no off-taste. Just two shakes on fruits, cereal or other food is equivalent in sweetening power to a teaspoonful of sugar. About twice as sweet as liquid *Sucaryl,* the granulated can also be used in cooking. The measuring cap filled to the line with granulated *Sucaryl* (1½ teaspoons) is the equivalent in sweetening power of 1 tablespoon of liquid *Sucaryl* or ½ cup of sugar. (For other sugar equivalencies, see "*Sucaryl*-Sugar Equivalencies," page 235.)

Sucaryl **Concentrate** is available in the calcium form in a 1-ounce plastic "squeeze" bottle. Two drops of this liquid concentrate equals 1 teaspoon of sugar in sweetening power. Convenient to carry in purse or pocket, the concentrate is preferred by many people for sweetening hot and cold beverages. Partly because of its highly concentrated sweetness, it is not as satisfactory for use in cooking as the less concentrated liquid *Sucaryl.*

Use of other sweeteners. If another brand of dietary sweetener is used in these recipes, remember that the sweetening power of different sweeteners varies widely. Some sweeteners are not as satisfactory for use in cooking as others. Certain saccharin-type sweeteners are not stable at cooking and freezing temperatures, sometimes developing an unpleasant, bitter aftertaste. *Always check the sweetener-sugar equivalency of other dietary sweeteners before substituting another sweetener in these recipes.*

Using *Sucaryl* in your own recipes. With the help of *Sucaryl,* calorie-wise cooks can slash away excess calories from many of their own favorite recipes. However, when making substitutions of *Sucaryl* for sugar in your own recipes, remember that *Sucaryl* has only the sweetening property of sugar. Generally, *Sucaryl* may be used to replace sugar in most pie fillings, puddings, custards, gelatin desserts and salads, salad dressings, relishes, pickles, and sauces. Use *Sucaryl,* too, in your home-canned and frozen fruits. You'll be delighted with the results.

When preparing certain foods, such as frozen desserts, jellies, candies and baked foods, remember that dietary sweeteners provide neither the bulking, stabilizing nor preservative properties of sugar. For recipes of these types, we suggest you use the special recipes included in this cookbook.

Where can you buy *Sucaryl?* *Sucaryl* is available in food stores and in drug stores. When shopping for dietetic foods and beverages, look for the name *Sucaryl* on the label. You'll find that these products have a natural-tasting sweetness.

Safety and effectiveness. Seldom, if ever, have consumer products been marketed with a background of nearly a decade of testing as were *Sucaryl* brand sweeteners when they were first made available to the public in 1950.

And although the safety of these products has been apparent day-in-and-day-out during eighteen years of widespread use by millions of persons, Abbott Laboratories continues to conduct scientifically controlled tests to further confirm safety and effectiveness.

The discovery leading to cyclamate sweeteners took place in 1937, but nine years of research and investigation passed before Abbott was satisfied that cyclamate, the basic ingredient of *Sucaryl* brand sweeteners, was safe for human consumption. Studies embraced both animals and human beings. (Experiments conducted by the Food and Drug Administration in Washington confirmed safety.) Cyclamate was subsequently approved by both the Council on Pharmacy and Chemistry and the Council on Foods and Nutrition of the American Medical Association.

In addition to the original nine years of research, Abbott has continued over the years to test *Sucaryl* brand sweeteners both in human beings and animals to establish further their safety and palatability. The Food and Drug Administration has acknowledged that sodium and calcium cyclamates are "generally recognized as safe" for use as non-nutritive sweeteners and places no limitations on their use.

Continued research has produced formula improvements that make it possible to sweeten to levels never before possible with a dietary sweetener, and virtually without aftertaste. As a result, countless numbers of people on sugar-restricted diets can enjoy natural-tasting, calorie-free sweetness in beverages and in cooked foods.

BEVERAGES

Coffee and Tea
Cocoa
Ginger-Mint Cooler
Lemonade
Berry Patch Lemonade
Claret Lemonade
Lemonade de Rosé
Spiced Orange Tea Cooler
Rum Eggnog
Pineapple Eggnog
Orange Eggnog
Banana Milk Shake

Chocolate Milk Shake

Strawberry Soda

Black and White Soda

Iced Coffee Float

Cranberry Frost

Frothy Syllabub

Golden Gate Punch

Orange Blossom Punch

Hot Spiced Harvest Punch

Hot Mocha Milk Punch

Spiced Cranberry Juice Cocktail

Coffee and Tea

For hot and iced drinks, sweeten to taste. One *Sucaryl* tablet or ⅛ teaspoon liquid *Sucaryl* is as sweet as one teaspoon of sugar. Tablets dissolve readily in hot beverages. In cold or iced drinks, use liquid *Sucaryl,* or dissolve tablets in a small amount of hot water before adding.

Cocoa

3 tablespoons cocoa	3 cups skim milk
1⅛ teaspoons liquid *Sucaryl*	

In top of double boiler, combine cocoa and *Sucaryl.* Blend in a small amount of the milk to make a smooth paste. Add remaining milk and heat thoroughly over boiling water. Add salt or cinnamon to taste.

Makes 4 servings, each 81 calories; 7 grams protein; 1.5 grams fat; 12 grams carbohydrate. (With sugar, 121 calories)

1 serving = 1 cup skim milk

Hot Spiced Mocha

⅓ cup cocoa	1 quart skim milk, scalded
1 tablespoon liquid *Sucaryl*	2 sticks cinnamon
1 cup strong coffee	

Place cocoa in large saucepan. Combine *Sucaryl* and coffee; gradually blend into cocoa, making a smooth paste. Add scalded milk and cinnamon sticks; bring mixture to the boil. Pour into mugs and, if desired, top with dollops of Low-Calorie Whipped Topping, page 178. Extra stick cinnamon may be used for stirrers.

Makes 6 servings, each 76 calories; 6 grams protein; 1.5 grams fat; 11.5 grams carbohydrate. (With sugar, 148 calories)

1 serving = 1 cup skim milk

Weight watchers should remember that calories in sugar-sweetened iced drinks mount up fast. In the following calorie-controlled coolers, all surplus calories which come with ordinary sweetening have been eliminated . . . a cool, reassuring thought on a summer's day.

Ginger-Mint Cooler

1 cup water
1 tablespoon liquid *Sucaryl*
¼ cup chopped mint leaves

½ cup lemon juice
2 cups orange juice
1 quart noncaloric ginger ale

Combine water, *Sucaryl* and mint leaves; bring to the boil. Strain and cool. At serving time, add remaining ingredients. Pour over crushed ice in tall glasses.

Makes 8 servings, each 30 calories; 0.5 grams protein; trace of fat; 8 grams carbohydrate. (With sugar, 85 calories)

1 serving = 1 fruit exchange

Lemonade

2 tablespoons fresh, strained
     lemon juice

⅜ teaspoon liquid *Sucaryl*
¾ cup water

Combine all ingredients; pour over ice in a tall glass. Garnish with slice of lemon.

Makes 1 serving, 8 calories; trace of protein; no fat; 2.5 grams carbohydrate. (With sugar, 62 calories)

Need not be calculated as exchanges.

Berry Patch Lemonade

1 cup lemon juice
2 tablespoons liquid *Sucaryl*
6 cups water

1 pint fresh strawberries, hulled
and puréed

Combine all ingredients; chill. Shake or stir before serving over ice in tall glasses. Garnish with whole strawberry and mint.

Makes 2 quarts or 8 servings, each 21 calories; 0.5 gram protein; trace of fat; 5.5 grams carbohydrate. (With sugar, 129 calories)

1 serving = ½ fruit exchange

Claret Lemonade

A distinguished drink . . . light and lovely for a summer luncheon.

½ cup lemon juice
1 tablespoon liquid *Sucaryl*
3 cups water
2 cups claret wine

Combine all ingredients. Pour over ice in goblets or tall glasses. Garnish with mint.

Makes 1½ quarts or 6 servings, each 61 calories; trace of protein; no fat; 2 grams carbohydrate. (With sugar, 133 calories)

Because of alcoholic content, consult physician before including in exchange-system diet.

Lemonade de Rosé

¾ cup lemon juice
¾ cup pineapple juice
1 bottle (3⅕ cups) rosé wine
2 tablespoons liquid *Sucaryl*
1 16-ounce bottle (2 cups)
noncaloric club soda

Combine all ingredients. Pour over crushed ice and garnish with lemon and mint.

Makes 14 half-cup servings, each 53 calories; trace of protein; no fat; 3 grams carbohydrate. (With sugar, 115 calories)

Because of alcoholic content, consult physician before including in exchange-system diet.

Spiced Orange Tea Cooler

Grated peel from 1 orange
3 whole cloves
6 whole allspice
1 cup boiling water
1 tablespoon liquid *Sucaryl*
1½ cups orange juice
¼ cup lime juice
1½ cups tea, chilled

Simmer grated orange peel and spices in boiling water 20 minutes; strain. Add *Sucaryl*, orange juice, lime juice and tea. Pour over ice in 4 tall glasses. Garnish with orange slice, cherry and mint.

Makes 4 servings, each 44 calories; 1 gram protein; trace of fat; 11.5 grams carbohydrate. (With sugar, 152 calories)

1 serving = 1 fruit exchange

Rum Eggnog

6 eggs, separated	1 tablespoon liquid *Sucaryl*
1 quart skim milk	½ cup rum

Beat egg yolks on high speed of mixer until thick. Gradually add milk, *Sucaryl* and rum; chill. Just before serving, fold in stiffly beaten egg whites.

Makes 8 1-cup servings, each 136 calories; 9 grams protein; 4 grams fat; 6.5 grams carbohydrate. (With sugar, 190 calories)

1 serving = 1 meat exchange
½ cup skim milk

Pineapple Eggnog

4 eggs, separated	1 tablespoon liquid *Sucaryl*
3 cups pineapple juice	1 cup skim milk

Beat egg yolks on high speed of mixer until thick. Gradually add pineapple juice, *Sucaryl* and milk. Chill. Just before serving, fold in stiffly beaten egg whites. Sprinkle with nutmeg, if desired.

Makes 8 1-cup servings, each 95 calories; 4.5 grams protein; 3 grams fat; 14 grams carbohydrate. (With sugar, 149 calories)

1 serving = 1½ fruit exchanges
½ meat exchange

Orange Eggnog

Substitute orange juice for pineapple juice in recipe above.

Makes 8 1-cup servings, each 90 calories; 5 grams protein; 3 grams fat; 12 grams carbohydrate. (With sugar, 144 calories)

1 serving = 1 fruit exchange
½ meat exchange

Banana Milk Shake

2 medium bananas
3 tablespoons orange juice
⅛ teaspoon salt
1 tablespoon liquid *Sucaryl*
⅛ teaspoon almond extract
2 cups skim milk

Combine all ingredients in blender or large bowl of mixer. Blend until foamy and smooth. Chill before serving.

Makes 4 servings, each 92 calories; 5 grams protein; trace of fat; 19 grams carbohydrate. (With sugar, 200 calories)

1 serving = 1½ fruit exchanges
½ cup skim milk

Chocolate Milk Shake

¼ cup cocoa
⅓ cup hot water
2 teaspoons liquid *Sucaryl*
1½ cups skim milk
1 cup low-calorie chocolate ice
milk

In blender, combine cocoa, hot water and *Sucaryl;* buzz to blend. Add milk and ice milk; buzz a few minutes until foamy.

Makes 2 servings, each 214 calories; 11 grams protein; 6.5 grams fat; 33 grams carbohydrate. (With sugar, 358 calories)

1 serving = 1 bread exchange
1 fat exchange
1½ cups skim milk

Strawberry Soda

¼ cup fresh lemon juice
½ cup fresh orange juice
1½ teaspoons liquid *Sucaryl*
½ cup sliced fresh strawberries

½ cup finely crushed ice
1 16-ounce bottle (2 cups)
  noncaloric club soda, chilled
1 pint dietary vanilla ice cream

Place fruit juices, *Sucaryl*, strawberries and crushed ice in blender; cover and blend until smooth. Divide among 4 tall chilled glasses. Fill with soda; top each with a scoop of ice cream; garnish with strawberries as desired. Serve at once.

Makes 4 servings, each 155 calories; 3.5 grams protein; 7 grams fat; 20.5 grams carbohydrate. (With sugar, 209 calories)

> *1 serving = 1 bread exchange*
> *2 fat exchanges*
> *1 fruit exchange*

Black and White Soda

⅓ cup hot water
¼ cup cocoa
2 teaspoons liquid *Sucaryl*
½ cup skim milk
1 cup dietary vanilla ice cream
Noncaloric club soda, chilled

Add hot water gradually to cocoa in small bowl to make a smooth paste. Blend in *Sucaryl* and skim milk. Divide between 2 tall glasses. Place ½ cup ice cream in each glass; fill with soda, stir and serve at once.

Makes 2 servings, each 193 calories; 6.5 grams protein; 10 grams fat; 24.5 grams carbohydrate. (With sugar, 337 calories)

> *1 serving = 1 bread exchange*
> *3 fat exchanges*
> *1 cup skim milk*

Iced Coffee Float

¼ cup instant coffee
⅓ cup boiling water
1 tablespoon liquid *Sucaryl*
½ teaspoon vanilla

Dash of salt
1 cup skim milk
1 pint dietary vanilla ice cream
Noncaloric soda water

Dissolve instant coffee in boiling water. Add *Sucaryl*, vanilla and salt; chill. Divide coffee mixture among four tall glasses. Add ¼ cup of the milk and ½ cup of the ice cream to each glass. Fill with soda water; stir and serve at once.

Makes 4 servings, each 153 calories; 5 grams protein; 7 grams fat; 17.5 grams carbohydrate. (With sugar, 261 calories)

> *1 serving = 1 bread exchange*
> *1 fat exchange*
> *¼ cup milk or ¼ cup skim milk*
> *+ ½ fat exchange*

Cranberry Frost

2 cups low-calorie cranberry
 juice cocktail
1 cup lemon juice
2 tablespoons liquid *Sucaryl*
2 16-ounce bottles (4 cups)
 noncaloric ginger ale, chilled
1 pint low-calorie lemon sherbet

Combine cranberry juice cocktail, lemon juice and *Sucaryl*; chill. At serving time, pour into 8 glasses; add ginger ale and sherbet.

Makes 8 servings, each 81 calories; 3 grams protein; 6 grams fat; 13 grams carbohydrate. (With sugar, 189 calories)

> *1 serving = ½ fruit exchange*
> *½ cup milk or ½ cup skim milk*
> *+ 1 fat exchange*

Frothy Syllabub

A festive holiday drink, syllabub is a near-cousin to eggnog but more nearly resembles a milk punch. In Richard Briggs' *New Art of Cookery,* published in Philadelphia in 1792, his receipt for "Syllabub under the Cow" begins this way:

> "Put a bottle of either red or white wine, ale or cyder, into a China bowl, sweeten it with sugar and grate in some nutmeg, then hold it under the cow, and milk into it till it has a fine froth at the top . . ."

The calorie-trimmed recipe which follows does not make use of Briggs' direct milking method, but achieves its characteristic frothy top by the addition of beaten egg whites.

3 tablespoons liquid *Sucaryl*
3 cups skim milk
2 cups sauterne
½ cup nonfat dry milk
½ cup ice water
2 egg whites
Nutmeg

In a large mixer bowl, combine 2 tablespoons of the *Sucaryl* with milk. Add wine, beating with electric mixer until frothy. Combine dry milk and ice water; beat on high speed of mixer until stiff peaks form; fold into wine mixture. Combine egg whites and remaining 1 tablespoon *Sucaryl;* beat until stiff peaks form. Pour punch into bowl. Top with mounds of beaten egg whites. Sprinkle with nutmeg.

Makes 1½ quarts or 12 half-cup servings, each 76 calories; 4.5 grams protein; no fat; 7 grams carbohydrate. (With sugar, 184 calories)

Because of alcoholic content, consult physician before including in exchange-system diet.

Golden Gate Punch

1 cup lemon juice
1 cup orange juice
1 cup grape juice
2 tablespoons liquid *Sucaryl*
4 cups water

Combine all ingredients and chill well. Serve over ice cubes, crushed ice or a ring mold of ice. Garnish with lemon or orange slices, as desired.

Makes 14 half-cup servings, each 24 calories; trace of protein; no fat; 6.5 grams carbohydrate. (With sugar, 86 calories)

1 serving = ½ fruit exchange

Orange Blossom Punch

3 cups orange juice
1 12-ounce can (1½ cups) low-
    calorie apricot nectar
½ cup lemon juice
1 tablespoon liquid *Sucaryl*
1 16-ounce bottle (2 cups)
    noncaloric ginger ale, chilled

Combine orange juice, apricot nectar, lemon juice and *Sucaryl;* chill well. Just before serving, add ginger ale. Serve from punch bowl garnished with orange slices.

Makes 14 half-cup servings, each 32 calories; 0.5 gram protein; trace of fat; 8 grams carbohydrate. (With sugar, 63 calories)

1 serving = 1 fruit exchange

Hot Spiced Harvest Punch

3 cups apple juice or cider
2 tablespoons liquid *Sucaryl*
4 sticks cinnamon

6 whole cloves
3 cups orange juice
1 cup lemon juice

Combine apple juice, *Sucaryl,* cinnamon and cloves. Bring to the boil and simmer about 5 minutes. Then add orange juice and lemon juice; bring just to the boil. Serve hot.

Makes 14 half-cup servings, each 54 calories; 0.5 gram protein; trace of fat; 14.5 grams carbohydrate. (With sugar, 115 calories)

1 serving = 1½ fruit exchanges

Hot Mocha Milk Punch

6 tablespoons cocoa
3 tablespoons instant coffee
2 tablespoons liquid *Sucaryl*
2 quarts skim milk

2 teaspoons rum extract*
¼ cup nonfat dry milk
¼ cup ice water

Combine cocoa, coffee and *Sucaryl* in a large saucepan or kettle. Slowly stir in milk. Heat over medium heat, stirring occasionally. When hot, remove from heat and add rum extract. Mix dry milk and ice water in bowl; beat until soft peaks form. Gently fold into hot cocoa mixture. Serve hot. Sprinkle with nutmeg, if desired.

Makes 16 half-cup servings, each 58 calories; 5 grams protein; 0.5 gram fat; 8.5 grams carbohydrate. (With sugar, 112 calories)

1 serving = ½ cup skim milk

* If rum is used in place of rum extract, count 35 calories for every half-ounce of rum. When 8 ounces of rum are added to above recipe, each serving would contain 93 calories. (With sugar, 147 calories)

Spiced Cranberry Juice Cocktail

A pleasantly sweet and tangy drink for those who prefer a non-alcoholic cocktail.

> 2 cups low-calorie cranberry
>   juice cocktail
> 3 whole cloves
> 1 stick cinnamon
> 2 tablespoons liquid *Sucaryl*
> ⅓ cup orange juice
> ¼ cup lemon juice
> ⅛ teaspoon salt

Combine cranberry juice, spices and *Sucaryl;* bring to the boil. Reduce heat and simmer 5 minutes. Remove from heat; add orange juice, lemon juice and salt. Chill and serve frosty cold.

Makes 5 half-cup servings, each 19 calories; 0.5 gram protein; trace of fat; 4 grams carbohydrates. (With sugar, 192 calories)

1 serving = ½ fruit exchange

BREADS

Apricot Oatmeal Bread
Cranberry-Orange Bread
Bran Bread
Cherry-Nut Party Bread
Chocolate Chip Tea Bread

Homemade hot breads often are named for the beverage most frequently served with them, for example, "coffee" cakes and "tea" breads. Whichever brew you're serving, it's an agreeable custom to accompany the beverage with "something sweet." Since the morning coffee break or the afternoon tea is an extra meal, make sure your "something sweet" is light and low in calories. All of the tempting breads featured here have been calorie-trimmed, yet taste just as delicious as their higher-calorie counterparts.

Completely sugar-free, these breads keep longer when wrapped and stored in the refrigerator. If you wish, bake extra loaves to keep in the freezer. At serving time, you can then reheat the bread to fragrant goodness, or slice thin and toast.

Cinnamon Coffee Cake

When you observe the fine texture and velvety crumb of this coffee cake, you'll find it hard to believe it contains no sugar whatsoever.

Topping
1 tablespoon melted butter
½ teaspoon cinnamon
½ teaspoon liquid *Sucaryl*
¼ cup toasted dry bread crumbs

Cake
2 cups sifted cake flour
3 teaspoons baking powder
¼ teaspoon salt
3 tablespoons soft butter
¾ cup skim milk
1 tablespoon liquid *Sucaryl*
4 drops yellow food coloring
1 egg

Preheat oven to 375°F. Grease an 8-inch round cake pan. Combine topping ingredients, stirring until blended; set aside. Sift flour, baking powder and salt into small mixer bowl. Cut in butter on low, then medium speed, 3 to 5 minutes, until mixture is completely blended and looks like fine corn meal. (This assures a fine grain.) Add ½ cup of the milk mixed with *Sucaryl* and coloring. Beat ½ minute on medium speed. (Batter will be stiff.) Add remaining milk and beat 1 minute longer. Add unbeaten egg and beat 1 minute more. Pour into prepared pan; sprinkle with cinnamon crumbs. Bake 20 minutes, or until cake springs back when lightly touched.

Makes 8 servings, each 169 calories; 4 grams protein; 6.5 grams fat; 23 grams carbohydrate. (With sugar, 232 calories)

1 serving = 1½ bread exchanges
1 fat exchange

Raised Coffee Cake

Cake
¼ cup skim milk
⅓ cup butter or margarine
1 teaspoon salt
1½ teaspoons liquid *Sucaryl*
2 packages active dry yeast
½ cup lukewarm water
2 eggs, beaten
3 cups sifted flour

Topping
⅓ cup chopped walnuts
½ teaspoon cinnamon
1 tablespoon melted butter
½ teaspoon liquid *Sucaryl*

Preheat oven to 400°F. Scald milk; add butter, salt and *Sucaryl;* stir until butter is melted. Cool to lukewarm (70°–90°F.). Dissolve yeast in lukewarm water; add to milk mixture. Add beaten eggs and flour; mix well. Spoon into greased 9-inch square cake pan. Let rise, covered, in warm place until double in bulk. Combine chopped walnuts, cinnamon, butter and *Sucaryl;* mix well and sprinkle over dough. Bake 20 minutes, or until done.

Makes 9 servings, each 257 calories; 7 grams protein; 12.5 grams fat; 29.5 grams carbohydrate. (With sugar, 289 calories)

1 serving = 2 bread exchanges
2½ fat exchanges

Casserole Raisin Bread

This round, fat loaf, studded with raisins, gets off to a quick start with the help of biscuit mix. Calorie count has been reduced nearly one-third.

2 cups biscuit mix
⅓ cup quick-cooking oatmeal
1 teaspoon baking powder
¼ teaspoon salt
½ cup raisins
1 egg, well beaten
1¼ cups skim milk
4½ teaspoons liquid *Sucaryl*

Preheat oven to 350°F. Combine biscuit mix, oatmeal, baking powder, salt and raisins. Combine remaining ingredients; add to dry ingredients all at once, blending well. Pour into a lightly greased 1-quart round casserole. Bake 50 to 60 minutes, or until done. Cool in casserole 10 minutes before turning out on wire rack.

Makes 15 servings, each 99 calories; 3 grams protein; 2.5 grams fat; 16.5 grams carbohydrate. (With sugar, 142 calories)

1 serving = 1 bread exchange
½ fat exchange

Banana Tea Bread

A really good tea bread can serve you well for many occasions. For breakfast, toast slices of this moist, delicately-flavored bread and spread with your favorite marmalade. For a salad luncheon, heat the bread and serve it thinly sliced with just a hint of butter. And for afternoon tea or for late evening snacks, prepare dainty sandwiches with a cottage cheese filling.

1¾ cups sifted flour	2 eggs, well beaten
2 teaspoons baking powder	2 tablespoons liquid *Sucaryl*
¼ teaspoon baking soda	1 teaspoon vanilla
½ teaspoon salt	2 medium bananas, mashed
¼ cup melted shortening	

Preheat oven to 350°F. Sift flour, baking powder, baking soda and salt together. Combine shortening, eggs, *Sucaryl* and vanilla. Add to flour mixture, stirring only until flour is moistened. Fold in mashed bananas. Turn into a well-greased loaf pan (7½ × 3¾ × 2½ inches). Bake 60 minutes, or until done.

Makes 12 servings, each 123 calories; 3 grams protein; 5 grams fat; 16 grams carbohydrate. (With sugar, 195 calories)

1 serving = 1 bread exchange
1 fat exchange

Orange Marmalade-Nut Bread

2 cups sifted flour
1½ teaspoons baking powder
½ teaspoon baking soda
¼ teaspoon salt
⅓ cup skim milk
1 egg

2 tablespoons melted butter
1 tablespoon liquid *Sucaryl*
½ cup low-calorie orange marmalade
¼ cup chopped walnuts

Preheat oven to 350°F. Combine flour, baking powder, baking soda and salt in a mixing bowl. Combine skim milk, egg, melted butter and *Sucaryl;* add to flour mixture, stirring only until all the flour is dampened. Fold in marmalade and nuts, mixing as little as possible. Spoon batter into a lightly greased loaf pan (7½ × 3¾ × 2¼ inches). Bake 50 minutes, or until done. Cool before slicing.

Makes 12 servings, each 111 calories; 3 grams protein; 4 grams fat; 15 grams carbohydrate. (With sugar, 147 calories)

1 serving = 1 bread exchange
1 fat exchange

Chocolate Chip Tea Bread

3 cups biscuit mix
¼ cup semi-sweet chocolate pieces (1½ ounces)
1¼ cups skim milk

4½ teaspoons liquid *Sucaryl*
1 egg
¼ teaspoon black walnut flavoring

Preheat oven to 350°F. Combine biscuit mix and chocolate pieces; blend to coat chocolate. Combine remaining ingredients, blending well. Pour into flour mixture, mixing well. Spoon into a greased loaf pan (8½ × 4½ × 2½ inches). Bake 75 minutes, or until done.

Makes 15 servings, each 125 calories; 3.5 grams protein; 4 grams fat; 18.5 grams carbohydrate. (With sugar, 168 calories)

1 serving = 1 bread exchange
1 fat exchange

Apricot Oatmeal Bread

2 cups biscuit mix
1 cup quick-cooking oatmeal
¼ teaspoon salt
1 teaspoon baking powder
⅓ cup dried apricots, chopped

¼ cup broken walnuts
4½ teaspoons liquid *Sucaryl*
1 egg, beaten
1¼ cups skim milk

Preheat oven to 350°F. Combine biscuit mix, oatmeal, salt, baking powder, apricots and walnuts. Combine *Sucaryl*, egg and milk, blending well. Add to dry ingredients, stirring only to mix. Turn into a greased loaf pan (8½ × 4½ × 2½ inches). Bake 60 minutes, or until done.

Makes 15 servings, each 120 calories; 3.5 grams protein; 4 grams fat; 17.5 grams carbohydrate. (With sugar, 163 calories)

1 serving = 1 bread exchange
1 fat exchange

Applesauce Tea Bread

2 cups sifted flour
3 teaspoons baking powder
½ teaspoon baking soda
½ teaspoon cinnamon
½ teaspoon salt

1 cup unsweetened applesauce
1 egg, beaten
4½ teaspoons liquid *Sucaryl*
2 tablespoons melted butter
½ teaspoon almond extract

Preheat oven to 350°F. Combine flour, baking powder, baking soda, cinnamon and salt. In large bowl, combine remaining ingredients, mixing well. Add flour mixture all at once, stirring only until flour is dampened. Spoon into a lightly greased loaf pan (7½ × 3¾ × 2¼ inches). Bake 60 minutes, or until done.

Makes 12 servings, each 98 calories; 2.5 grams protein; 2.5 grams fat; 16 grams carbohydrate. (With sugar, 152 calories)

1 serving = 1 bread exchange
½ fat exchange

Bran Bread

1½ cups sifted flour
4½ teaspoons baking powder
½ teaspoon salt
¾ cup whole bran cereal,
  crumbled slightly
1 cup skim milk
4½ teaspoons liquid *Sucaryl*
1 egg
¼ cup salad oil

Preheat oven to 350°F. Sift together the flour, baking powder and salt. Add bran, blending well. Combine remaining ingredients; add to flour mixture, stirring just to blend. Turn into a greased loaf pan (7½ × 3¾ × 2¼ inches). Bake 70 minutes, or until done.

Makes 12 servings, each 113 calories; 3 grams protein; 5.5 grams fat; 14.5 grams carbohydrate. (With sugar, 167 calories)

1 serving = 1 bread exchange
1 fat exchange

Cherry-Nut Party Bread

3 cups biscuit mix
10 maraschino cherries,
  drained and chopped
¼ cup chopped walnuts
1¼ cups skim milk
2 tablespoons liquid *Sucaryl*
1 egg, well beaten

Preheat oven to 350°F. In large bowl, combine biscuit mix, cherries and nuts. Combine remaining ingredients; add to dry ingredients all at once, beating well. Pour into a greased loaf pan (8½ × 4½ × 2½ inches). Bake 75 minutes, or until done.

Makes 15 servings, each 136 calories; 3.5 grams protein; 4.5 grams fat; 20.5 grams carbohydrate. (With sugar, 194 calories)

1 serving = 1 bread exchange
1 fat exchange
½ fruit exchange

Cranberry-Orange Bread

2 cups sifted flour
1½ teaspoons baking powder
½ teaspoon salt
½ teaspoon baking soda
½ cup orange juice
1 egg, slightly beaten
2 tablespoons melted shortening
2 tablespoons liquid *Sucaryl*
2 tablespoons hot water
1 cup whole cranberries
½ cup chopped walnuts

Preheat oven to 350°F. Combine flour, baking powder, salt and soda in a large mixing bowl. Combine orange juice, egg, melted shortening, *Sucaryl* and hot water, blending well. Pour over the dry ingredients and mix only until they are moistened. Fold in the cranberries and nuts. Spoon into a well-greased loaf pan (7½ × 3¾ × 2¼ inches). Bake 90 minutes, or until golden brown on top. Cool slightly before removing from pan.

Makes 12 servings, each 133 calories; 3.5 grams protein; 6 grams fat; 17 grams carbohydrate. (With sugar, 205 calories)

1 serving = 1 bread exchange
1 fat exchange

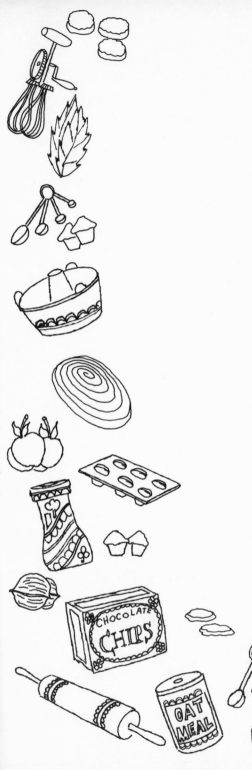

CAKES, TORTES,

Plain Sponge Cake
Coffee Sponge Cake
Spicy Sponge Cake
Orange Sponge Cake
Chocolate Sponge Cake
Orange Chiffon Cake
Chiffon Cake
Golden Spice Cake

COOKIES

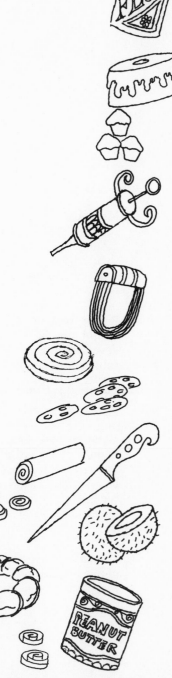

Walnut Torte
Pecan Torte
Peanut Butter Cookies
Oatmeal Cookies
Chocolate Chip Cookies
Coconut Macaroons
Applesauce Cookies
Chocolate Banana Drop Cookies

Most women are surprised to learn that it's possible to bake certain cakes and cookies without using any sugar. All of the cakes, tortes and cookies which follow are remarkably good, and should be especially welcomed by those who, for dietary reasons, must curb their intake of sugar. All are completely sugar-free.

Baking without sugar can present problems, of course, and should not be attempted unless you use recipes especially developed for calorie-free sweetening. Do not attempt to make substitutions in your own recipes. As has been pointed out earlier, calorie-free sweeteners have only the sweetening property of sugar. They provide neither the bulking, stabilizing nor preservative qualities of sugar.

We do not recommend using calorie-free sweetening for cakes requiring a fat and sugar emulsion (where sugar and shortening are creamed together), as in butter cakes. You should, however, have notably good results with these sugar-free recipes for sponge-type cakes, chiffon-type cakes and cakes made by the muffin method of mixing (see Cinnamon Coffee Cake, page 35).

The cake recipes, when carefully followed, will produce cakes of fine texture and reasonably good volume. The crumb will be exceptionally tender, and the flavor will be pleasant and sweet.

Cake batters will nearly fill the pans, and will rise only slightly during baking. Expect the top of the cakes to be puffed and somewhat uneven, similar in appearance to the top of a baked soufflé.

Here are a few hints which we've found important to successful sugar-free cake baking: Have eggs at room temperature for best volume when beaten. For the sponge cakes, be sure to beat the egg yolks the full 5 minutes in order to incorporate sufficient air for maximum volume. It's equally important to avoid overmixing (which will break down the foam) when folding the batter into the beaten egg whites.

Incidentally, baked foods of all sorts will keep longer if they are wrapped and refrigerated.

Plain Sponge Cake

7 eggs, separated
½ cup water
1 teaspoon grated lemon rind
3 tablespoons liquid *Sucaryl*
1 tablespoon lemon juice

1 teaspoon vanilla
1½ cups sifted cake flour
¼ teaspoon salt
¾ teaspoon cream of tartar

Preheat oven to 325°F. Have eggs at room temperature for best volume when beaten. On high speed of mixer, beat egg yolks until thick and lemon-colored, 5 minutes. Combine water, lemon rind, *Sucaryl*, lemon juice and vanilla. Combine sifted cake flour and salt; beat into yolks alternately with liquid. Beat egg whites until foamy; add cream of tartar and beat until stiff peaks form. Fold batter *gently* into the stiffly beaten egg whites. Pour into an ungreased 9-inch tube pan. Bake 65 minutes, or until done. Invert cake to cool.

Makes 12 servings, each 91 calories; 4.5 grams protein; 3.5 grams fat; 10 grams carbohydrate. (With sugar, 199 calories)

1 serving = ½ bread exchange
½ meat exchange

Coffee Sponge Cake

Prepare Plain Sponge Cake recipe, omitting lemon rind and vanilla; add 1 tablespoon instant coffee to the sifted cake flour and salt.

Makes 12 servings, each 91 calories; 4.5 grams protein; 3.5 grams fat; 10 grams carbohydrate. (With sugar, 199 calories)

1 serving = ½ bread exchange
½ meat exchange

Spicy Sponge Cake

Prepare Plain Sponge Cake recipe, omitting lemon rind and vanilla; add 1 teaspoon cinnamon, ½ teaspoon nutmeg, ½ teaspoon cloves and ½ teaspoon allspice to the sifted cake flour and salt.

Makes 12 servings, each 91 calories; 4.5 grams protein; 3.5 grams fat; 10 grams carbohydrate. (With sugar, 199 calories)

1 serving = ½ bread exchange
½ meat exchange

Orange Sponge Cake

Prepare Plain Sponge Cake recipe, substituting ½ cup orange juice for the water and 1 tablespoon grated orange rind for the lemon rind; increase lemon juice to 2 tablespoons and decrease vanilla to ½ teaspoon.

Makes 12 servings, each 95 calories; 4.5 grams protein; 3.5 grams fat; 11.5 grams carbohydrate. (With sugar, 204 calories)

1 serving = ½ bread exchange
½ meat exchange

Chocolate Sponge Cake

Prepare Plain Sponge Cake recipe, omitting lemon rind; substitute ½ cup cocoa for ½ cup of the cake flour.

Makes 12 servings, each 89 calories; 4.5 grams protein; 4.5 grams fat; 9 grams carbohydrate. (With sugar, 197 calories)

*1 serving = ½ bread exchange
½ meat exchange*

Chiffon Cake

2¼ cups sifted cake flour
3 teaspoons baking powder
1 teaspoon salt
½ cup salad oil
7 eggs, separated
½ cup water
3 tablespoons liquid *Sucaryl*
2 teaspoons grated lemon rind
1 teaspoon vanilla
½ teaspoon cream of tartar

Preheat oven to 325°F. Have eggs at room temperature for best volume when beaten. In small mixer bowl, sift together the flour, baking powder and salt. Make well in center; add oil, egg yolks, water, *Sucaryl*, lemon rind and vanilla. Beat until smooth. In large mixer bowl, beat egg whites until foamy; add cream of tartar and beat until very stiff peaks form. *Gently* fold batter into stiffly beaten egg whites until just blended. (*Do not stir.*) Turn into an ungreased 9-inch tube pan. Bake 65 minutes, or until done. Invert cake to cool.

Makes 12 servings, each 194 calories; 5 grams protein; 12.5 grams fat; 15 grams carbohydrate. (With sugar, 302 calories)

*1 serving = 1 bread exchange
2 fat exchanges
½ meat exchange*

Orange Chiffon Cake

Prepare Chiffon Cake recipe, substituting ½ cup orange juice for the water. Omit lemon rind and vanilla, and add 3 tablespoons grated orange rind.

Makes 12 servings, each 199 calories; 5 grams protein; 12.5 grams fat; 16 grams carbohydrate. (With sugar, 307 calories)

1 serving = 1 bread exchange
2 fat exchanges
½ meat exchange

Golden Spice Cake

2¼ cups sifted cake flour	½ cup salad oil
3 teaspoons baking powder	7 eggs, separated
1½ teaspoons cinnamon	1 cup cooked or canned pumpkin
¾ teaspoon cloves	3 tablespoons liquid *Sucaryl*
¾ teaspoon nutmeg	½ teaspoon cream of tartar
¼ teaspoon salt	

Preheat oven to 325°F. Have eggs at room temperature for best volume when beaten. In small mixer bowl, sift together the flour, baking powder, spices and salt. Make a well in center; add oil, egg yolks, pumpkin and *Sucaryl;* beat until smooth. In a large mixer bowl, beat egg whites until foamy; add cream of tartar and beat until very stiff peaks form. *Gently* fold batter into stiffly beaten egg whites until just blended. (*Do not stir.*) Turn into an ungreased 9-inch tube pan. Bake 65 minutes, or until done. Invert cake to cool.

Makes 12 servings, each 200 calories; 5 grams protein; 12.5 grams fat; 16.5 grams carbohydrate. (With sugar, 308 calories)

1 serving = 1 bread exchange
2 fat exchanges
½ meat exchange

Walnut Torte

3 eggs, separated
½ teaspoon orange extract
1½ teaspoons liquid *Sucaryl*
⅛ teaspoon salt
1 teaspoon lemon juice
2 teaspoons liquid *Sucaryl*
1 cup English walnuts, ground

Preheat oven to 350°F. Combine egg yolks, orange extract, 1½ teaspoons *Sucaryl* and salt in bowl; beat until yolks are very light and fluffy. Beat egg whites until foamy; add lemon juice and 2 teaspoons *Sucaryl;* beat until peaks form. Fold egg whites and ground nuts into yolk mixture. Pour into a well-greased 8-inch square cake pan. Bake about 35 minutes, or until done.

Makes 9 servings, each 98 calories; 3.5 grams protein; 9 grams fat; 2 grams carbohydrate. (With sugar, 154 calories)

1 serving = 2 fat exchanges
½ meat exchange

Pecan Torte

Prepare Walnut Torte recipe, substituting 1 cup pecans, ground, for the walnuts.

Makes 9 servings, each 109 calories; 3 grams protein; 10.5 grams fat; 1.5 grams carbohydrate. (With sugar, 165 calories)

1 serving = 2 fat exchanges
½ meat exchange

Peanut Butter Cookies

¼ cup butter
½ cup peanut butter
2 tablespoons liquid *Sucaryl*
⅓ cup skim milk
1 egg
1 teaspoon vanilla
1 cup sifted flour
1 teaspoon baking powder
¼ teaspoon salt

Preheat oven to 375°F. Combine butter, peanut butter and *Sucaryl*; blend well. Add milk combined with egg and vanilla. Sift flour, baking powder and salt together, and add, blending well. Drop by rounded teaspoonfuls onto greased cookie sheet. Flatten with a fork dipped in water. Bake about 10 minutes.

Makes 48 cookies, each 34 calories; 1 gram protein; 2.5 grams fat; 2.5 grams carbohydrate. (With sugar, 52 calories)

5 cookies = 1 bread exchange
2 fat exchanges
½ meat exchange

Oatmeal Cookies

1¼ cups quick-cooking oatmeal
⅔ cup melted butter
2 eggs, beaten
2 tablespoons liquid *Sucaryl*
1½ cups sifted flour
2 teaspoons baking powder
½ teaspoon salt
½ cup skim milk
1 teaspoon vanilla

Preheat oven to 400° F. Place oatmeal in large mixing bowl. Combine butter, eggs and *Sucaryl*, blending well. Add to oatmeal. Combine dry ingredients; add alternately with the combined milk and vanilla. Drop by rounded teaspoonfuls onto ungreased baking sheet. Bake 12 minutes.

Makes 48 cookies, each 47 calories; 1 gram protein; 3 grams fat; 4 grams carbohydrate. (With sugar, 65 calories)

4 cookies = 1 bread exchange
2 fat exchanges
½ meat exchange

Chocolate Chip Cookies

> 1 cup sifted flour
> ½ teaspoon baking soda
> ¼ teaspoon salt
> ½ cup butter
> 4 teaspoons liquid *Sucaryl*
> ½ teaspoon vanilla
> 1 egg, beaten
> ½ cup semi-sweet chocolate
>   pieces (3 ounces)

Preheat oven to 375°F. Sift together the dry ingredients. Cream butter; add *Sucaryl*, vanilla and egg, blending well. Add flour mixture and beat well. Stir in the chocolate pieces. Drop by level teaspoonfuls onto a lightly greased baking sheet. Bake 8 to 10 minutes.

Makes 36 cookies, each 48 calories; 0.5 gram protein; 3.5 grams fat; 3.5 grams carbohydrate. (With sugar, 64 calories)

4 cookies = 1 bread exchange
3 fat exchanges

Chocolate Banana Drop Cookies

2¼ cups sifted flour
2 teaspoons baking powder
¾ teaspoon salt
¼ teaspoon baking soda
⅔ cup butter
1 teaspoon vanilla
2 tablespoons water
2 eggs
2 tablespoons liquid *Sucaryl*
2 medium bananas, mashed
1 square unsweetened chocolate, melted

Preheat oven to 400°F. Sift together the flour, baking powder, salt and soda. Cream together the butter, vanilla, water, eggs, and *Sucaryl* until creamy and smooth. Add the sifted flour mixture and mashed bananas alternately, mixing until well blended. (Do not overmix.) Blend in melted chocolate. Place by rounded teaspoonfuls on greased cookie sheet. Bake 12 to 15 minutes.

Makes 54 cookies, each 45 calories; 1 gram protein; 2.5 grams fat; 4.5 grams carbohydrate. (With sugar, 61 calories)

5 cookies = 1 bread exchange
2½ fat exchanges
1 fruit exchange

Applesauce Cookies

1¾ cups sifted flour
½ teaspoon salt
1 teaspoon cinnamon
½ teaspoon nutmeg
½ teaspoon cloves
1 teaspoon baking soda

½ cup butter
2 tablespoons liquid *Sucaryl*
1 egg
1 cup unsweetened applesauce
⅓ cup raisins
1 cup whole bran cereal

Preheat oven to 375°F. Sift together the flour, salt, cinnamon, nutmeg, cloves and baking soda. Mix butter, *Sucaryl* and egg until light and fluffy. Then add flour mixture and applesauce alternately, mixing well after each addition. Fold in raisins and cereal. Drop by level tablespoonfuls onto greased cookie sheet, about 1 inch apart. Bake 18 minutes, or until golden brown.

Makes 48 cookies, each 40 calories; 0.5 gram protein; 2 grams fat; 5 grams carbohydrate. (With sugar, 58 calories)

> 5 cookies = 1 bread exchange
> 2 fat exchanges
> 1 fruit exchange

Coconut Macaroons

> 2 cups dried shredded coconut
> 2 tablespoons cake flour
> ¼ teaspoon baking powder
> 2 egg whites
> ¼ teaspoon cream of tartar
> 1 tablespoon liquid *Sucaryl*

Preheat oven to 350°F. Combine coconut, cake flour and baking powder. Beat egg whites until foamy; add cream of tartar and *Sucaryl;* beat until peaks form. Fold egg whites into coconut mixture. Drop by rounded teaspoonfuls onto greased cookie sheet. Bake 12 to 15 minutes, or until golden brown. (If you like macaroons moist, cool and store in a covered container. Macaroons become crisp when left uncovered.)

Makes 24 macaroons, each 32 calories; 0.5 gram protein; 2 grams fat; 3 grams carbohydrate. (With sugar, 50 calories)

> 2 macaroons = ½ bread exchange
> 1 fat exchange

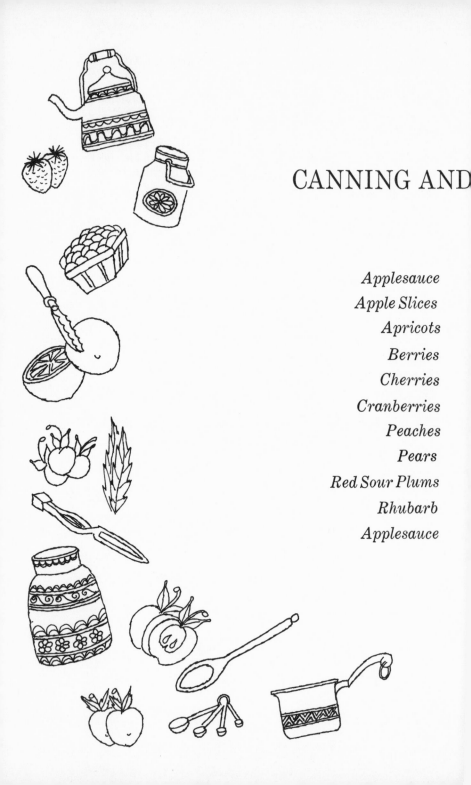

CANNING AND

Applesauce
Apple Slices
Apricots
Berries
Cherries
Cranberries
Peaches
Pears
Red Sour Plums
Rhubarb
Applesauce

FREEZING OF FRUITS

Apple Slices
Apricots
Berries
Cherries
Cranberries
Peaches
Pears
Red Sour Plums
Rhubarb
Strawberries

When you use *Sucaryl* instead of sugar in home canning or freezing of fruits, you eliminate 864 calories for every cup of sugar ordinarily required to achieve the same sweet taste. Best of all, you will find that fruits packed with calorie-free sweetening rate just as high in texture, color, flavor and sweetness as those packed in a sugar syrup. In fact, many people prefer *Sucaryl*-sweetened preserved fruits to those sweetened with sugar.

It is recommended that some fruits be dropped into a 3% brine in order to prevent discoloration before packing. To make this brine, dissolve 2 tablespoons of salt in 1 gallon of water. Some recipes also recommend the addition of ascorbic acid (vitamin C) in order to prevent surface darkening. Ascorbic acid may be obtained at your drugstore.

(*Water-Bath Method of Canning*)

APPLESAUCE: Select firm, tart apples. Wash, quarter, core and remove all bruised or decayed parts. Drop into 3% brine; drain. Cook in small amount of water until soft. Press through sieve or colander to remove skins. Measure. Add 2 teaspoons liquid *Sucaryl* (or 16 *Sucaryl* tablets) to each cup of sauce. Bring to the boil. Pack boiling hot into clean, hot jars, filling jars to within ½ inch of top. Cap tightly. Process in boiling-water bath, 25 minutes.

APPLE SLICES: Select firm, tart apples. Wash, pare, core and slice into 3% brine; drain. Simmer 5 minutes in small amount of water; drain, saving juice. Pack hot into clean, hot jars. Add 2 teaspoons liquid *Sucaryl* (or 16 *Sucaryl* tablets) and ⅛ teaspoon ascorbic acid to each cup of juice. (Add water to juice if necessary to obtain full cup measure.) Pour boiling sweetened juice over fruit, filling jars to within ½ inch of top. Cap tightly. Process in boiling-water bath, 15 minutes.

APRICOTS: Select firm, ripe fruit. Peel, if desired, halve and pit. (If fruit is peeled, drop into 3% brine; drain.) Pack into clean, hot jars. Add 1 tablespoon liquid *Sucaryl* (or 24 *Sucaryl* tablets) and ⅛ teaspoon ascorbic acid to each cup of boiling water. Pour boiling sweetened water over fruit, filling jars to within ½ inch of top. Cap tightly. Process in boiling-water bath, 20 minutes.

BERRIES: (*All berries except strawberries and cranberries.*) Wash berries, pick over carefully and drain. Pack into clean, hot jars. Add 1 tablespoon liquid *Sucaryl* (or 24 *Sucaryl* tablets) to each cup of boiling water. Pour boiling sweetened water over berries, filling jars to within ½ inch of top. Cap tightly. Process in boiling-water bath, 20 minutes.

CHERRIES: (*All varieties.*) Wash, stem and pit, if desired. Pack into clean, hot jars. *For sour cherries,* add 2 tablespoons liquid *Sucaryl* (or 48 *Sucaryl* tablets) to each cup of boiling water. *For sweet cherries,* add 1 tablespoon liquid *Sucaryl* (or 24 *Sucaryl* tablets) to each cup of boiling water. Pour boiling sweetened water over cherries, filling jars to within ½ inch of top. Cap tightly. Process in boiling-water bath, 20 minutes.

CRANBERRIES: Wash and stem berries. For every 2 cups of berries, add 2 tablespoons liquid *Sucaryl* and 1 cup water. Boil 3 minutes. Pack into clean, hot jars to within ½ inch of top. Cap tightly. Process in boiling-water bath, 10 minutes.

PEACHES: Select firm, ripe peaches. Remove skins and pits. Halve or slice into a 3% brine; drain. Pack into clean, hot jars. Add 1 tablespoon liquid *Sucaryl* (or 24 *Sucaryl* tablets) and ⅛ teaspoon ascorbic acid to each cup of boiling water. Pour boiling sweetened water over peaches, filling jars to within ½ inch of top. Cap tightly. Process in boiling-water bath, 20 minutes.

PEARS: Pare, halve and core pears. Drop into 3% brine; drain. Precook pears in small amount of water for 3 minutes; drain, saving juice. Pack hot fruit into clean, hot jars. Add 2 teaspoons liquid *Sucaryl* (or 16 *Sucaryl* tablets) to each cup of hot juice. (Add more sweetened water, if necessary, to get enough liquid to fill jars.) Pour boiling sweetened juice over pears, filling jars to within ½ inch of top. Cap tightly. Process in boiling-water bath, 25 minutes.

RED SOUR PLUMS: Wash plums and prick skin with needle to prevent bursting. Pack into clean, hot jars. Add 1 tablespoon liquid *Sucaryl* (or 24 *Sucaryl* tablets) to each cup of boiling water. Pour boiling sweetened water over plums, filling jars to within ½ inch of top. Cap tightly. Process in boiling-water bath, 20 minutes.

RHUBARB: Wash stalks; do not peel. Cut into 1-inch pieces. Pack cold into clean, hot jars. Add 2 tablespoons liquid *Sucaryl* (or 48 *Sucaryl* tablets) to each cup of boiling water. Pour boiling sweetened water over rhubarb, filling jars to within ½ inch of top. Cap tightly. Process in boiling-water bath, 20 minutes.

(*Home Method of Freezing Fruits*)

APPLESAUCE: Select firm, tart apples. Wash, quarter, core and remove all bruised or decayed parts. Drop into 3% brine; drain. Cook in a small amount of water until soft. Put through sieve or colander to remove skins. Measure. Add 2 teaspoons liquid *Sucaryl* (or 16 *Sucaryl* tablets dissolved in small amount of boiling water) to each cup of sauce. Pack into containers, leaving ½ inch head space. Seal; cool; freeze.

APPLE SLICES: Select firm, tart apples. Wash, pare, core and slice into 3% brine; drain. Simmer 3 minutes in small amount of water; drain, saving juice. Pack into containers, leaving ½ inch head space. Add 2 teaspoons liquid *Sucaryl* (or 16 *Sucaryl* tablets) and ⅛ teaspoon ascorbic acid to each cup of hot juice. (Add boiling water to juice, if necessary, to obtain full cup measure.) Cover fruit with sweetened juice. Top with crushed freezer paper to keep fruit immersed in juice. Seal; cool; freeze.

APRICOTS: Select firm, ripe fruit. Peel, if desired, halve and pit. (If fruit is peeled, drop into 3% brine; drain.) Pack into containers, leaving ½ inch head space. Add 1 tablespoon liquid *Sucaryl* (or 24 *Sucaryl* tablets dissolved in small amount of boiling water) and ⅛ teaspoon ascorbic acid to each cup of water. Cover fruit with sweetened water. Top with crushed freezer paper to keep fruit immersed in juice. Seal and freeze.

BERRIES: (*Except cranberries and strawberries*) Wash berries, pick over carefully and drain. Place in large bowl. For 6 cups berries, add 1 tablespoon liquid *Sucaryl* (or 24 *Sucaryl* tablets dissolved in small amount of boiling water) to ¼ cup water. Pour sweetened water over berries. Pack into containers, leaving ½ inch head space. Seal and freeze.

CHERRIES: (*All varieties*) Wash, stem and pit. Pack into containers, leaving ½ inch head space. *For sour cherries,* add 2 tablespoons liquid *Sucaryl* (or 48 *Sucaryl* tablets dissolved in small amount of boiling water) to each cup water. *For sweet cherries,* add 1 tablespoon liquid *Sucaryl* (or 24 *Sucaryl* tablets dissolved in small amount of boiling water) to each cup water. Cover fruit with sweetened water. Seal and freeze.

CRANBERRIES: Wash, drain and pack dry without sweetening. Before cooking, sweeten with 1 tablespoon liquid *Sucaryl* (or 24 *Sucaryl* tablets) for each cup of cranberries.

PEACHES: Select firm, ripe peaches. Remove skins and pits. Slice into a 3% brine; drain. Pack into containers, leaving ½ inch head space. Add 1 tablespoon liquid *Sucaryl* (or 24 *Sucaryl* tablets dissolved in small amount of boiling water) and ⅛ teaspoon ascorbic acid to each cup water. Cover fruit with sweetened water. Top with crushed freezer paper to keep fruit immersed in juice. Seal and freeze.

PEARS: Pare, halve and core pears. Drop into 3% brine; drain. Precook pears in small amount of water for 3 minutes; drain, saving juice. Pack into containers, leaving ½ inch head space. Add 2 teaspoons liquid *Sucaryl* (or 16 *Sucaryl* tablets) to each cup of hot juice. (Add boiling water to juice, if necessary, to obtain full cup measure.) Cover fruit with sweetened juice. Top with crushed freezer paper to keep fruit immersed in juice. Seal; cool; freeze.

RED SOUR PLUMS: Wash, halve and pit. Pack into containers, leaving ½ inch head space. Add 4½ teaspoons liquid *Sucaryl* (or 36 *Sucaryl* tablets dissolved in small amount of boiling water) to each cup water. Pour sweetened water over plums. Seal and freeze.

RHUBARB: Wash stalks; do not peel. Cut into 1-inch pieces. Pack into containers, leaving ½ inch head space. Seal and freeze. Before cooking, sweeten with 1½ teaspoons liquid *Sucaryl* (or 12 *Sucaryl* tablets) for every cup of fruit.

STRAWBERRIES: Wash and stem strawberries; pick over carefully; drain. Pack dry without sweetening. Before using, sweeten with 1 teaspoon liquid *Sucaryl* (or 8 *Sucaryl* tablets dissolved in small amount of boiling water) for each cup of berries.

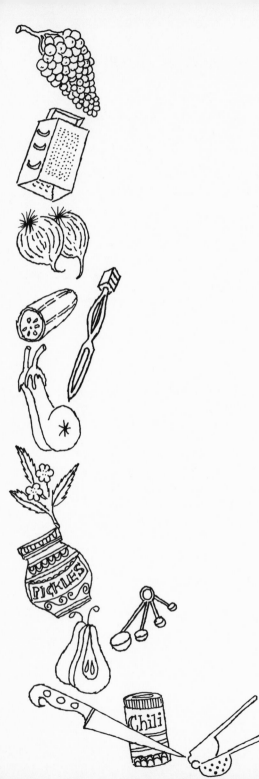

CONDIMENTS

Crisp Cucumber Pickle
Mustard Pickle
Zucchini Pickles
Curried Pickle Slices
Red Beet Relish
Garden Vegetable Relish
Pickled Onion Rings
Pickled Beets
Mustard Beans
Corn Chowder Relish
Crispy Winter Relish
Cranberry-Apple Relish
Pear Chutney

Jellied Cranberry Sauce

Spiced Apples

Spiced Peaches

Curried Fruit Bake

Chili Sauce

Dutch Mustard Sauce

Tomato Catsup

Hot Barbecue Sauce

Golden Barbecue Sauce

Sweet'n'Sour Marinade

California Raisin Sauce

Apricot Sauce

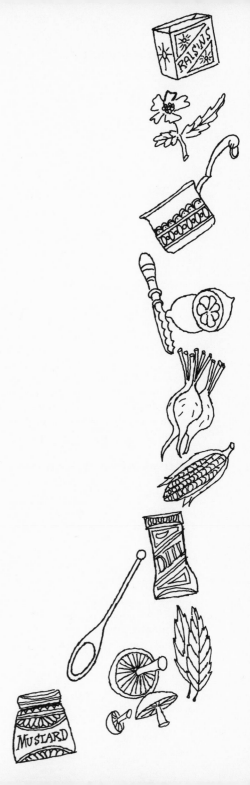

Leaf through early American cookbooks and you'll invariably find a generous section of "rules for relishes and oddments." Homemade relishes were considered indispensable to the meal, and were served as "side dishes" at luncheon and dinner to add spirit and zest to the main course.

If you're conscientious about calories, you'll do well to check the calorie counts of your favorite condiments. That special "added touch" to a meal—a tangy relish, a piquant chutney, a savory sauce—often adds a forbiddingly high number of extra unwanted calories.

Most relishes and meat sauces carry a high calorie tab because they contain a lot of sugar. If you concoct your own homemade condiments, however, you can often trim calories to a fraction of the usual count, simply by substituting calorie-free sweetening for sugar. In tune with the times, all of the pickles, relishes and meat sauces which follow have been calorie-streamlined so that dieters and nondieters alike can enjoy their tantalizing goodness.

Crisp Cucumber Pickle

6 firm cucumbers
¼ cup salt
1½ tablespoons liquid *Sucaryl*
¼ cup water

2 cups white vinegar
2 tablespoons mixed pickling spice

Wash and dry cucumbers; cut into strips to fit half-pint jars. Place in large bowl; sprinkle with salt and let stand overnight. Rinse and drain well several times. Combine *Sucaryl*, water and vinegar in a large kettle; bring to the boil. Add pickling spice tied in a cheesecloth bag. Add cucumbers. Reduce heat; simmer 15 minutes. Pack cucumbers into clean, hot half-pint jars. Heat liquid again to boiling; pour over pickles in jars. Seal at once.

Makes 6 half-pints, each jar 34 calories; 1.5 grams protein; trace of fat; 9.5 grams carbohydrate. (With sugar, 142 calories)

Need not be calculated as exchanges.

Mustard Pickle

3 cups raw cauliflower buds
2 cucumbers, pared and finely chopped
2 green peppers, seeded and cut into chunks
1 pound small white onions, peeled
2⅔ tablespoons salt

4 cups cold water
3 tablespoons dry mustard
1½ teaspoons turmeric
2 tablespoons liquid *Sucaryl*
2 cups vinegar
⅓ cup flour
1 cup water

Combine vegetables, salt and the 4 cups water in large kettle; let stand overnight; drain. Add spices, *Sucaryl* and vinegar. Bring to the boil; boil 15 minutes. Make a smooth paste of the flour and 1 cup water; add to vegetables and cook 5 minutes longer. Ladle into clean, hot, half-pint jars; seal at once.

Makes 6 half-pints, each ¼-cup serving 23 calories; 1 gram protein; trace of fat; 5.5 grams carbohydrate. (With sugar, 58 calories)

1 serving = 1 "A" vegetable exchange

Zucchini Pickles

1 quart cider vinegar	1 teaspoon turmeric
4 tablespoons liquid *Sucaryl*	4 pounds zucchini, sliced
½ cup salt	¼-inch thick
2 teaspoons celery seed	1 pound (4 large) yellow
2 teaspoons mustard seed	onions, thinly sliced

In large kettle, combine vinegar, *Sucaryl*, salt, celery seed, mustard seed and turmeric. Bring to the boil; remove from heat and add sliced vegetables. Cover and let stand 1 hour. Heat to the boil; reduce heat and simmer 3 minutes. Ladle into clean, hot jars; seal at once.

Makes 4½ pints, each ¼-cup serving 16 calories; 0.5 gram protein; no fat; 4.5 grams carbohydrate. (With sugar, 64 calories)

1 serving = ½ "B" vegetable exchange

Curried Pickle Slices

2½ pounds (8 cups) cucumbers,	2 teaspoons curry powder
thinly sliced	2 teaspoons mixed pickling spice
2 medium onions, thinly sliced	1 teaspoon celery seed
1 tablespoon salt	1 teaspoon mustard seed
2 cups vinegar	½ teaspoon pepper
8 teaspoons liquid *Sucaryl*	
1 green pepper, coarsely chopped	

In large kettle, combine cucumbers, onions and salt; cover with ice water and let stand 3 hours. Drain well. In large kettle, combine remaining ingredients; add cucumber and onion slices. Bring just to the boil. Ladle into clean, hot jars; seal at once.

Makes 3 pints, each ¼-cup serving 11 calories; 0.5 gram protein; no fat; 3 grams carbohydrate. (With sugar, 59 calories)

If no more than ¼ cup is used, need not be calculated as exchanges.

Red Beet Relish

4 cups chopped, raw cabbage
4 cups chopped, cooked beets
1 teaspoon salt
1 cup prepared horseradish

½ teaspoon white pepper
4 tablespoons liquid *Sucaryl*
2 cups vinegar

Combine all ingredients in large kettle. Cover; bring to the boil. Ladle into clean, hot jars; seal at once.

Makes 4 pints, each ¼-cup serving 18 calories; 0.5 gram protein; no fat; 4.5 grams carbohydrate. (With sugar, 72 calories)

1 serving = ½ "B" vegetable exchange

Garden Vegetable Relish

10 medium green peppers, cleaned and quartered
1 pound (½ medium head) cabbage, trimmed
1 pound carrots, without tops, scraped
1 pound (4 large) onions, peeled and quartered

3 cups white vinegar
½ cup water
3 tablespoons liquid *Sucaryl*
3 tablespoons salt
1 tablespoon mustard seed
1 tablespoon celery seed

Wash vegetables; put through coarse blade of food chopper; drain well. Combine with remaining ingredients in large kettle. Bring to the boil; reduce heat and simmer about 5 minutes. Pack into clean, hot jars; seal at once.

Makes 6 pints, each ¼-cup serving 15 calories; 0.5 gram protein; no fat; 3.5 grams carbohydrate. (With sugar, 42 calories)

1 serving = ½ "B" vegetable exchange

Corn Chowder Relish

¾ teaspoon celery seed	¼ teaspoon salt
½ teaspoon dry mustard	1 cup white vinegar
¼ teaspoon turmeric	2 cups sweet corn, cut from cob
2 tablespoons flour	1 cup chopped cabbage
1 tablespoon liquid *Sucaryl*	1 green pepper, finely chopped

In large saucepan, combine spices, flour, *Sucaryl* and salt. Blend in vinegar to make a smooth paste. Add vegetables. Bring to the boil; reduce heat and simmer 30 minutes. Pack into clean, hot half-pint jars. Seal at once.

Makes 4 half-pints, each ¼-cup serving 24 calories; 0.5 gram protein; trace of fat; 6 grams carbohydrate. (With sugar, 51 calories)

1 serving = ½ bread exchange

Pear Chutney

4 fresh pears	½ teaspoon ginger
¾ cup raisins	¼ teaspoon salt
¼ cup chopped green pepper	¼ teaspoon cloves
1 cup vinegar	¼ teaspoon allspice
4 tablespoons liquid *Sucaryl*	2 sticks cinnamon

Pare, core and coarsely chop pears. Combine with remaining ingredients in large kettle. Bring to the boil, then cook over medium heat until pears are tender and mixture has thickened slightly (about 1 hour). Spoon into clean, hot half-pint jars. Seal at once.

Makes 3 half-pints, each ¼-cup serving 61 calories; 0.5 gram protein; trace of fat; 16 grams carbohydrate. (With sugar, 205 calories)

1 serving = 1½ fruit exchanges

No need to get out the canning kettles and jars when you make up a batch of these sweet and spicy instant relishes. All five of the following recipes can be freshly prepared in a matter of minutes, then left to marinate in the refrigerator.

Pickled Onion Rings

> 2 medium onions, thinly sliced   ¼ teaspoon salt
> ½ cup cider vinegar   1 stick cinnamon
> ½ cup water   1 teaspoon whole cloves
> ¾ teaspoon liquid *Sucaryl*

Separate onion slices into rings. Combine remaining ingredients; bring to the boil; reduce heat and simmer 5 minutes. Pour over onion rings. Cover and refrigerate overnight. Drain before serving.

Makes 1½ cups, each ¼-cup serving 19 calories; 0.5 gram protein; no fat; 4.5 grams carbohydrate. (With sugar, 37 calories)

1 serving = ½ "B" vegetable exchange

Pickled Beets

> 1 1-pound can sliced beets   ⅛ teaspoon pepper
> ½ cup cider vinegar   2 whole cloves
> ¾ teaspoon liquid *Sucaryl*   1 bay leaf
> ½ teaspoon salt

Drain beets. In saucepan, combine the liquid with remaining ingredients. Bring to the boil; reduce heat and simmer 5 minutes. Pour over beets. Cover and refrigerate overnight. Drain before serving.

Makes 1½ cups, each ¼-cup serving 28 calories; 0.5 gram protein; no fat; 7 grams carbohydrate. (With sugar, 46 calories)

1 serving = 1 "B" vegetable exchange

Crispy Winter Relish

1 cup finely chopped apples
1 cup finely shredded cabbage
½ cup finely diced celery
1 tablespoon chopped green pepper
1 tablespoon chopped pimiento
3 tablespoons vinegar
2 teaspoons liquid *Sucaryl*
½ teaspoon salt
¼ teaspoon ginger
¼ teaspoon dry mustard
Dash of cayenne

Combine apples and vegetables. Combine vinegar, *Sucaryl*, salt and spices, blending well. Pour over apples and vegetables, tossing lightly. Refrigerate at least 1 hour.

Makes 2 cups, each ¼-cup serving 17 calories; 0.5 gram protein; trace of fat; 5 grams carbohydrate. (With sugar, 53 calories)

1 serving = ½ fruit exchange

Cranberry-Apple Relish

2 cups raw cranberries
¼ cup raisins
½ cup diced apple
¼ cup chopped walnuts
2 tablespoons liquid *Sucaryl*
½ teaspoon lemon juice

Put cranberries and raisins through coarse blade of food chopper. Add remaining ingredients, mixing well. Chill in refrigerator several hours.

Makes 1¾ cups, each ¼-cup serving 64 calories; 1 gram protein; 3 grams fat; 10 grams carbohydrate. (With sugar, 188 calories)

1 serving = 1 fat exchange
1 fruit exchange

Mustard Beans

½ teaspoon instant minced onion
¼ teaspoon salt
1 1-pound can yellow wax
  beans, drained
½ cup cider vinegar
3 tablespoons prepared mustard
1 tablespoon liquid *Sucaryl*

In saucepan, combine all ingredients except beans; bring to the boil. Add drained beans; simmer uncovered 5 minutes; cool. Cover; refrigerate overnight. Serve as a relish, as a meat accompaniment or in a salad.

Makes 1½ cups, each ¼-cup serving 22 calories; 1 gram protein; 0.5 gram fat; 4.5 grams carbohydrate. (With sugar, 94 calories)

1 serving = 1 "A" vegetable exchange

Jellied Cranberry Sauce

2 cups raw cranberries
1 cup water
1 envelope unflavored gelatin
¼ cup cold water
2 tablespoons liquid *Sucaryl*

Combine cranberries and the 1 cup water; cook until skins pop. Soften gelatin in the ¼ cup cold water. Add cooked cranberries, stirring to dissolve gelatin.* Add *Sucaryl*. Pour into a 1-pound can or 2-cup mold. Chill until set. Slice to serve.

Makes 8 ¼-cup servings, each 18 calories; 1 gram protein; trace of fat; 3 grams carbohydrate. (With sugar, 126 calories)

If no more than ¼ cup is used, need not be calculated as exchanges.

* *To make plain cranberry jelly, force cooked cranberries through food mill or strainer; add to softened gelatin and proceed as directed.*

Spiced Apples

4 medium cooking apples
1 cup cider
3 tablespoons liquid *Sucaryl*
2 sticks cinnamon
½ teaspoon whole cloves
⅛ teaspoon ground allspice
⅛ teaspoon ground ginger
⅛ teaspoon nutmeg
1½ tablespoons lemon juice
1 tablespoon cornstarch

Pare, core and slice apples; place in cold water. Combine cider, *Sucaryl*, spices and lemon juice; bring to the boil. Add drained apple slices and cook until soft but not broken. Remove apples. Make a paste of the cornstarch and a small amount of water. Add to spiced cider; cook and stir over low heat until mixture thickens slightly. Pour over apples. Serve warm or chilled.

Makes 6 half-cup servings, each 77 calories; 0.5 gram protein; 0.5 gram fat; 20.5 grams carbohydrate. (With sugar, 293 calories)

1 serving = 2 fruit exchanges

Spiced Peaches

> 2 1-pound cans low-calorie
>   peach halves
> 4 teaspoons liquid *Sucaryl*
> 2 sticks cinnamon
> 1 teaspoon whole cloves
> ½ teaspoon ground allspice
> ½ cup vinegar

Drain peaches and combine liquid with *Sucaryl*, spices and vinegar. Boil 5 minutes. Add peaches and simmer 5 minutes. Let fruit chill in liquid overnight. Drain and serve as meat accompaniment.

Makes 10 servings, each 26 calories; 0.5 gram protein; trace of fat; 6.5 grams carbohydrate. (With sugar, 83 calories)

1 serving = ½ fruit exchange

Curried Fruit Bake

Low-calorie, diet-sweetened canned fruits are enjoying an enthusiastic reception from the diet-conscious public, and are often considered to have a truer fruit flavor than the regular syrup pack. Three *Sucaryl*-sweetened canned fruits are featured in this sweet and spicy meat accompaniment.

> 1 14-ounce can low-calorie
>   sliced pineapple
> 1 1-pound can low-calorie pear halves
> 1 1-pound can low-calorie
>   apricot halves
> 8 maraschino cherries
> ¼ cup melted butter
> 1½ tablespoons liquid *Sucaryl*
> 3 teaspoons curry powder

Preheat oven to 325°F. Drain fruit; arrange in a shallow 1½-quart casserole. Combine melted butter, *Sucaryl* and curry powder; pour mixture over fruit. Bake about 60 minutes. Serve hot as accompaniment to meat or poultry.

Makes 8 servings, each 144 calories; 0.5 gram protein; 5.5 grams fat; 22.5 grams carbohydrate. (With sugar, 225 calories)

1 serving = 1 fat exchange
2 fruit exchanges

Chili Sauce

> 4 pounds ripe tomatoes
> 2 green peppers, chopped
> 2 sweet red peppers, chopped
> 1½ cups chopped celery
> 1½ cups chopped onion
> 3 tablespoons liquid *Sucaryl*
> 1 tablespoon Tabasco
> 1 tablespoon salt
> 1½ cups cider vinegar
> 1 stick cinnamon
> 1 teaspoon whole cloves
> 1½ teaspoons mustard seed
> 1½ teaspoons celery seed

Pour boiling water over tomatoes; peel and chop. In large heavy kettle, combine chopped tomatoes, green and red peppers, celery, onion, *Sucaryl*, Tabasco, salt and vinegar. Tie spices in cheesecloth bag and add to tomato mixture. Bring to the boil; reduce heat and simmer, stirring occasionally, until of desired consistency (about 5 hours). Pour into clean, hot half-pint jars; seal at once.

Makes 6 half-pints, each tablespoon 6 calories; trace of protein; no fat; 1.5 grams carbohydrate. (With sugar, 19 calories)

Need not be calculated as exchanges.

Dutch Mustard Sauce

1 tablespoon liquid *Sucaryl*
¼ cup dry mustard
¼ teaspoon salt
2 eggs, well beaten

½ cup skim milk
½ cup vinegar
2 tablespoons butter

In top of double boiler, combine *Sucaryl*, mustard and salt. Blend in beaten eggs, milk and vinegar; cook over hot water, beating constantly with rotary beater, *only* until mixture thickens. (If overcooked, mixture will curdle.) Remove from heat and blend in butter. Serve hot or cold on corned beef brisket, ham, fresh pork, roast beef, frankfurters, cold cuts. Also excellent as salad dressing.

Makes 1½ cups, each tablespoon 17 calories; 0.5 gram protein; 1.5 grams fat; 0.5 gram carbohydrate. (With sugar, 35 calories)

If only 1 tablespoon is used, need not be calculated as exchanges. If larger amounts are used, 2 tablespoons = ½ fat exchange.

Tomato Catsup

6 pounds (18 medium) ripe tomatoes
1 cup chopped onions
1 tablespoon salt.
2 tablespoons liquid *Sucaryl*
1½ teaspoons celery seed
½ teaspoon mustard seed
¼ teaspoon allspice
½ stick cinnamon
¾ cup vinegar
1½ teaspoons paprika

Wash, drain, core and chop tomatoes. Cook with onions until

soft; press through a sieve. Boil rapidly until reduced to half. Add salt, *Sucaryl* and spices tied in a bag. Boil until thick. Add vinegar and paprika. Boil 5 minutes longer, or until as thick as desired. Pour into 2 clean half-pint jars; seal.

Makes 2 half-pint jars, each tablespoon 18 calories; 1 gram protein; trace of fat; 3.5 grams carbohydrate. (With sugar, 45 calories)

1 tablespoon = ½ "A" vegetable exchange

Hot Barbecue Sauce

We've found that meats basted with a *Sucaryl* barbecue sauce are less apt to burn than when sugar is an ingredient.

1 tablespoon butter	½ cup catsup
1 medium onion, chopped	1 beef bouillon cube
1 teaspoon dry mustard	1 teaspoon cider vinegar
1 tablespoon cornstarch	½ teaspoon Tabasco
1 cup water	½ teaspoon celery salt
1½ teaspoons liquid *Sucaryl*	½ teaspoon paprika
1½ teaspoons Worcestershire sauce	

In small saucepan, melt butter over low heat until frothy. Add onion and sauté until soft and golden in color. Blend in mustard and cornstarch to make a smooth paste. Add remaining ingredients; bring to the boil. Reduce heat and simmer, stirring occasionally, for at least 60 minutes. Use to baste hot dogs, hamburgers, spareribs or chicken.

Makes 1¼ cups sauce, each tablespoon 16 calories; trace protein; 0.5 gram fat; 2.5 grams carbohydrate. (With sugar, 26 calories)

Need not be calculated as exchanges.

Golden Barbecue Sauce

⅓ cup prepared mustard
1 tablespoon liquid *Sucaryl*
2 tablespoons Worcestershire sauce
½ cup vinegar
¼ teaspoon Tabasco
⅛ teaspoon savory
⅛ teaspoon basil
⅓ cup sauterne

In small saucepan, combine all ingredients, beating until well blended; keep warm on side of grill and use to baste chicken, Rock Cornish game hens or turkey.

Makes 1⅛ cups sauce, each tablespoon 8 calories; trace of protein; 0.5 gram fat; 1 gram carbohydrate. (With sugar, 28 calories)

Need not be calculated as exchanges.

Sweet 'n' Sour Marinade (for Shish Kebabs)

1 cup soy sauce
½ cup vinegar
½ cup pineapple juice
½ cup unsweetened pineapple juice
1 tablespoon liquid *Sucaryl*
½ teaspoon salt
½ teaspoon garlic powder

Combine all ingredients. Marinate beef or lamb cubes in mixture for at least 4 hours. Use also to baste meat while cooking. Makes 2 cups sauce, each tablespoon 6 calories; no protein; trace of fat; 1.5 gram carbohydrate. (With sugar, 20 calories)

Need not be calculated as exchanges.

California Raisin Sauce

½ cup white raisins
1 cup water
2 tablespoons cornstarch
⅔ cup low-calorie grape jelly
⅔ cup orange juice
1 tablespoon liquid *Sucaryl*
⅛ teaspoon salt
⅛ teaspoon allspice

Rinse raisins. Blend water into cornstarch. Add remaining ingredients, including the raisins. Cook over medium heat, stirring constantly, until thick and clear. Serve hot with baked ham or sliced tongue.

Makes 2⅔ cups, each ⅓-cup serving 48 calories; 0.5 gram protein; no fat; 12 grams carbohydrate. (With sugar, 102 calories)

1 serving = 1 fruit exchange

Apricot Sauce

2 8¼-ounce cans low-calorie   1 tablespoon liquid *Sucaryl*
   apricot halves   1½ teaspoons minced onion
1 tablespoon cornstarch   1 teaspoon soy sauce

Drain 1 can of the apricot halves and set fruit aside. Blend this liquid into the cornstarch in small saucepan. Force remaining can of apricots, including liquid, through food mill; blend with remaining ingredients into the cornstarch mixture. Cook over medium heat, stirring constantly, until clear and thick. Remove from heat. Add apricot halves. Serve hot with roast duck or ham.

Makes 1½ cups, each ¼-cup serving 33 calories; 0.5 gram protein; no fat; 7 grams carbohydrate. (With sugar, 105 calories)

1 serving = ½ fruit exchange

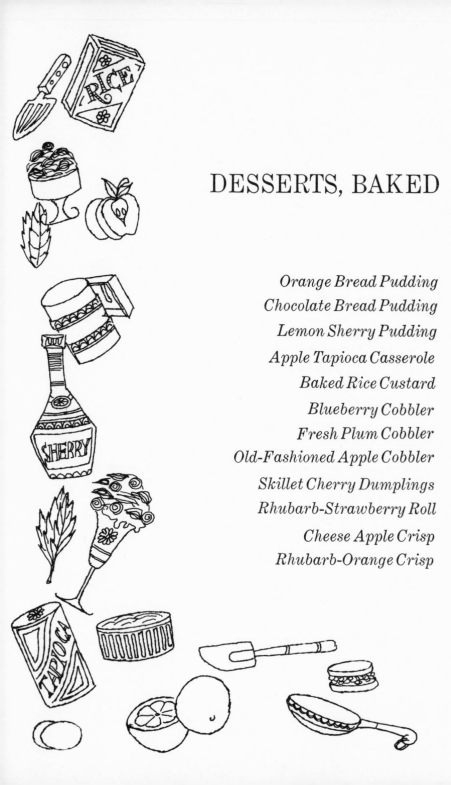

DESSERTS, BAKED

Orange Bread Pudding
Chocolate Bread Pudding
Lemon Sherry Pudding
Apple Tapioca Casserole
Baked Rice Custard
Blueberry Cobbler
Fresh Plum Cobbler
Old-Fashioned Apple Cobbler
Skillet Cherry Dumplings
Rhubarb-Strawberry Roll
Cheese Apple Crisp
Rhubarb-Orange Crisp

Cherry-Berry Crumble

Dieter's Strawberry Shortcake

Baked Custard

Vanilla Pots de Crème

Coffee Pots de Crème

Almond Pots de Crème

Chocolate Pots de Crème

Baked Vanilla Soufflé

Baked Chocolate Soufflé

Baked Apricot Soufflé

Baked Brandy Soufflé

Baked Orange Soufflé

Dieter's Strawberry Shortcake

Biscuit-type Shortcake
1 cup sifted flour
1½ teaspoons baking powder
Pinch of salt
3 tablespoons butter
1 egg
¾ teaspoon liquid *Sucaryl*
¼ cup skim milk

Strawberry Sauce
4 cups hulled strawberries
2 tablespoons liquid *Sucaryl*
2 tablespoons water

Preheat oven to 450°F. Combine flour, baking powder and salt. Cut in butter until of consistency of coarse corn meal. Combine remaining ingredients; stir into flour mixture. Knead gently about 10 times. Roll ¼ inch thick on lightly floured board. Cut into 6 3-inch circles. Place on ungreased baking sheet; bake 12 to 15 minutes. Cool.

Crush 1 cup of the strawberries; add *Sucaryl* and water. Pour over remaining whole berries and chill.

Split biscuits and fill with sauce; top with remaining sauce. If desired, garnish with Low-Calorie Whipped Topping, page 178.

Makes 6 servings, each 169 calories; 4 grams protein; 7 grams fat; 23 grams carbohydrate. (With sugar, 331 calories)

1 serving = 1 bread exchange
1 fat exchange
1 fruit exchange

Orange Bread Pudding

Even bread pudding can be classified as diet fare when made this sweet and low-calorie way.

4 slices bread, cubed	¼ teaspoon salt
3 eggs, beaten	¼ cup dried shredded coconut
4½ teaspoons liquid *Sucaryl*	2 tablespoons raisins
1½ cups orange juice	

Preheat oven to 350°F. Lightly butter a 4-cup casserole. Place bread cubes in casserole. Combine remaining ingredients; pour over bread and mix lightly. Place in pan of hot water and bake 40 minutes, or until a knife inserted near center comes out clean.

Makes 6 servings, each 131 calories; 5 grams protein; 4.5 grams fat; 18.5 grams carbohydrate. (With sugar, 239 calories)

1 serving = 1 bread exchange
½ fruit exchange
½ meat exchange

Chocolate Bread Pudding

4 slices bread, cubed	¼ teaspoon salt
3 cups warm skim milk	3 eggs, separated
6 tablespoons cocoa	4½ teaspoons liquid *Sucaryl*

Preheat oven to 350°F. Place bread cubes in large bowl. Gradually add milk to cocoa, making a smooth mixture. Pour over bread; let stand 15 minutes. Combine salt, egg yolks and *Sucaryl;* stir lightly into bread mixture. Beat egg whites until peaks form; fold into bread mixture. Pour into a lightly buttered 6-cup casserole (or 6 individual lightly buttered custard cups). Place in a pan of hot water. Bake 45 to 60 minutes, or until set.

Makes 6 servings, each 145 calories; 9.5 grams protein; 5 grams fat; 18 grams carbohydrate. (With sugar, 253 calories)

1 serving = 1 bread exchange
½ meat exchange
½ cup skim milk

Apple Tapioca Casserole

3 large apples, pared, cored
  and cut into eighths
⅓ cup quick-cooking tapioca
2 cups water
2 tablespoons liquid *Sucaryl*
2 tablespoons lemon juice
1 teaspoon mace

Preheat oven to 375°F. Arrange apple slices in a shallow 4-cup baking dish. In a small saucepan, combine remaining ingredients. Bring to the boil, stirring constantly. Pour over apple slices; bake 20 minutes. Remove from oven and serve warm.

Makes 6 servings, each 90 calories; 0.5 gram protein; 0.5 gram fat; 23 grams carbohydrate. (With sugar, 234 calories)

1 serving = 1 bread exchange
1 fruit exchange

Lemon Sherry Pudding

When baked, this delightful dessert forms two layers . . . a sweet and tangy lemon pudding on the bottom, a light-textured cake on top.

2 tablespoons flour
½ teaspoon cinnamon
½ teaspoon salt
1 egg plus 2 egg yolks
3 tablespoons sherry
2 tablespoons lemon juice
1 cup skim milk
4½ teaspoons liquid *Sucaryl*
2 egg whites, stiffly beaten

Preheat oven to 350°F. Combine flour, cinnamon and salt in a small bowl. Combine egg plus yolks, sherry, lemon juice, milk and *Sucaryl*. Add to dry ingredients, beating well. Fold in stiffly beaten egg whites. Pour into a lightly buttered 4-cup casserole. Set in a pan of hot water and bake 55 to 60 minutes. Serve warm or chilled.

Makes 4 servings, each 109 calories; 7 grams protein; 4 grams fat; 7.5 grams carbohydrate. (With sugar, 271 calories)

1 serving = ½ bread exchange
1 meat exchange

Baked Rice Custard

This classic from the South should be slow-baked the old-fashioned way, and tastes best when served still warm and fragrant from the oven.

> 3 eggs, well beaten
> 1½ cups skim milk
> 1 tablespoon liquid *Sucaryl*
> ¼ teaspoon salt
> ½ teaspoon vanilla
> ¾ cup cooked rice
> 3 tablespoons raisins

Preheat oven to 350°F. Blend together the eggs, skim milk, *Sucaryl*, salt and vanilla. Stir in cooked rice and raisins. Pour into a 4-cup casserole. Place casserole in a pan of hot water. Bake, uncovered, 60 minutes, stirring after one half hour of baking. Serve hot.

Makes 6 servings, each 98 calories; 6 grams protein; 3 grams fat; 12.5 grams carbohydrate. (With sugar, 170 calories)

1 serving = 1 bread exchange
½ meat exchange

Blueberry Cobbler

3 cups blueberries
1 tablespoon liquid *Sucaryl*
2 tablespoons quick-cooking
tapioca
¾ cup water
1¼ cups biscuit mix
½ cup skim milk
½ teaspoon liquid *Sucaryl*

Preheat oven to 350°F. Combine blueberries, the 1 tablespoon *Sucaryl*, tapioca and water; turn into a shallow 6-cup baking dish. Combine biscuit mix, milk and ½ teaspoon of *Sucaryl*, mixing only until flour is dampened. With spoon, form into 6 biscuits on top of the berries. Bake 30 to 40 minutes, or until the biscuits are golden brown and the berries bubbling hot.

Makes 6 servings, each 163 calories; 3.5 grams protein; 3.5 grams fat; 30.5 grams carbohydrate. (With sugar, 247 calories)

1 serving = 1½ bread exchanges
1 fat exchange
1 fruit exchange

Fresh Plum Cobbler

3 cups fresh plum halves
½ cup water
4 teaspoons liquid *Sucaryl*
1½ cups biscuit mix
⅔ cup skim milk
½ teaspoon liquid *Sucaryl*

Preheat oven to 350°F. Combine plum halves, water and 4 teaspoons of *Sucaryl* in a saucepan; cook until fruit is just tender. Pour into a shallow 6-cup baking dish. Combine biscuit mix, skim milk and ½ teaspoon *Sucaryl*, stirring just enough to mix. Drop by tablespoonfuls onto fruit mixture. Bake 40 minutes, or until biscuits are brown. Serve warm with milk, if desired.

Makes 6 servings, each 179 calories; 4 grams protein; 4 grams fat; 33 grams carbohydrate. (With sugar, 287 calories)

> *1 serving = 1½ bread exchanges*
> *1 fat exchange*
> *1 fruit exchange*

Old-Fashioned Apple Cobbler

> **5 cups sliced raw apples**
> **3 tablespoons cornstarch**
> **¾ teaspoon nutmeg**
> **½ teaspoon cinnamon**
> **2 tablespoons liquid *Sucaryl***
> **3 tablespoons lemon juice**
> **1½ cups water**
> **1 cup biscuit mix**
> **¼ cup skim milk**
> **⅜ teaspoon liquid *Sucaryl***

Preheat oven to 450°F. Place apples in a shallow 6-cup casserole. In saucepan, combine cornstarch, nutmeg, cinnamon, 2 tablespoons *Sucaryl* and lemon juice to make a smooth paste. Add water; cook over medium heat, stirring constantly until thickened. Pour over apples in casserole. Combine biscuit mix, milk and ⅜ teaspoon *Sucaryl*. Mix with a fork to form a soft dough. Drop by spoonfuls onto apples. Bake 15 to 20 minutes, or until apples are tender and biscuits are brown.

Makes 6 servings, each 171 calories; 2.5 grams protein; 3 grams fat; 35 grams carbohydrate. (With sugar, 324 calories)

> *1 serving = 1 bread exchange*
> *1 fat exchange*
> *2 fruit exchanges*

Skillet Cherry Dumplings

2 tablespoons quick-cooking tapioca
1 cup water
1 1-pound can water-pack sour
  red cherries
1 tablespoon liquid *Sucaryl*

Dumplings
1 cup sifted flour
2 teaspoons baking powder
⅛ teaspoon salt
2 tablespoons butter
⅓ cup skim milk
1½ teaspoons liquid *Sucaryl*
½ teaspoon vanilla

In heavy skillet, combine tapioca and water; add cherries and
Sucaryl. Simmer gently 5 to 10 minutes, stirring occasionally,
until sauce is thickened. *To make dumplings,* combine flour,
baking powder and salt in small bowl. Cut butter into dry ingredients. Combine milk, *Sucaryl* and vanilla. Add to flour mixture and stir to make a stiff batter. Drop by tablespoonfuls onto
cherries in skillet. Cover and steam gently for 20 to 25 minutes.

Makes 6 servings, each 152 calories; 3 grams protein; 4 grams
fat; 26.5 grams carbohydrate. (With sugar, 260 calories)

1 serving = 1 bread exchange
1 fat exchange
1 fruit exchange

Rhubarb-Strawberry Roll

Here's a tempting dessert to make at the first glimpse of satiny pink stalks of rhubarb and luscious red strawberries at the fruit counter.

2 cups rhubarb, cut into 1-inch pieces
2 cups strawberries, sliced
1 cup water
2 tablespoons liquid *Sucaryl*
2 tablespoons cornstarch
2 cups biscuit mix
⅔ cup skim milk

Preheat oven to 450°F. In a medium saucepan, combine rhubarb, strawberries, water and *Sucaryl*. Cover; simmer until tender, about 5 minutes. Drain, reserving liquid; set fruit aside.

In a small saucepan, blend a small amount of the liquid with cornstarch, making a smooth paste. Blend in remaining liquid. Cook over medium heat, stirring constantly, until mixture thickens; remove from heat.

Combine biscuit mix and milk; blend well. Roll dough into a rectangular sheet about ¼ inch thick. Cover with fruit; roll as for jelly roll. Cut into 8 slices. Place in a shallow baking dish. Pour sauce over rolls. Bake 35 minutes, or until nicely browned. Serve warm or cold and with milk, if desired.

Makes 8 servings, each 155 calories; 4 grams protein; 4 grams fat; 26.5 grams carbohydrate. (With sugar, 263 calories)

1 serving = 1½ bread exchanges
½ fruit exchange
1 fat exchange

Cherry-Berry Crumble

1 1-pound can water-pack red
sour cherries
1 10-ounce package frozen unsweetened blueberries
¼ cup quick-cooking tapioca
1½ tablespoons liquid *Sucaryl*
2 tablespoons lemon juice

Topping
8 small graham crackers,
crushed
1 teaspoon grated lemon rind
1 tablespoon melted butter
¾ teaspoon liquid *Sucaryl*

Preheat oven to 350°F. Drain cherries; measure liquid and add enough water to make 1½ cups. Combine cherries and blueberries in a shallow 4-cup casserole. In a saucepan, combine tapioca, *Sucaryl,* lemon juice and cherry liquid. Cook over medium heat, stirring constantly, until tapioca is cooked and mixture is thickened. Pour over fruit in casserole. Bake 10 minutes. Remove from oven. Combine all ingredients for topping; sprinkle over partially cooked fruit; return to oven and bake 10 minutes longer.

Makes 6 servings, each 124 calories; 1.5 grams protein; 3 grams fat; 25.5 grams carbohydrate. (With sugar, 250 calories)

1 serving = 1 bread exchange
1 fruit exchange

Cheese Apple Crisp

Favorite of dieters and nondieters alike will be this easy-to-make but scrumptious casserole dessert, to be served warm from the oven on a chilly evening.

4 medium apples, cored and
sliced
¼ cup water
½ teaspoon lemon juice
4½ teaspoons liquid *Sucaryl*

½ cup flour
½ teaspoon salt
½ teaspoon cinnamon
3 tablespoons butter
½ cup grated Cheddar cheese

Preheat oven to 350°F. Place sliced apples in a deep pie plate or a shallow baking dish. Combine water, lemon juice and *Sucaryl;*

pour over apples. Combine flour, salt and cinnamon; cut in butter until of consistency of coarse meal; sprinkle over apples. Cover with grated cheese. Bake 30 to 40 minutes, or until apples are tender.

Makes 6 serving, each 171 calories; 3.5 grams protein; 9 grams fat; 20.5 grams carbohydrate. (With sugar, 279 calories)

1 serving = 1 fat exchange
2 fruit exchanges
½ meat exchange

Rhubarb-Orange Crisp

Although rhubarb in itself is low in calories (1 cup diced raw rhubarb, 19 calories), this tangy fruit normally requires a lot of sugar to make it palatable. (One cup of cooked rhubarb with sugar added has a calorie count of 383 calories!) Why add those extra calories when it's so easy to make the fruit pleasurably sweet this calorie-trimmed way?

4 cups diced rhubarb
8 teaspoons liquid *Sucaryl*
16 small graham crackers, crushed
1 tablespoon grated orange rind

1 teaspoon grated lemon rind
¼ cup melted butter
½ cup orange juice

Preheat oven to 350°F. Sprinkle rhubarb with *Sucaryl*; set aside. Combine graham cracker crumbs, orange and lemon rinds and butter, blending well. In a shallow 4-cup casserole, alternate layers of rhubarb and crumbs, ending with crumbs. Pour orange juice over top. Bake 40 to 45 minutes, or until rhubarb is tender.

Makes 6 servings, each 125 calories; 1.5 grams protein; 8.5 grams fat; 12.5 grams carbohydrate. (With sugar, 317 calories)

1 serving = 1 bread exchange
2 fat exchanges

Baked Custard

> 3 eggs
> 2 teaspoons liquid *Sucaryl*
> ⅛ teaspoon salt
> 1 teaspoon vanilla
> 2 cups skim milk, scalded

Preheat oven to 300°F. Lightly butter 5 custard cups. Combine eggs, *Sucaryl*, salt and vanilla; mix well. Gradually add scalded milk, blending well. Pour into custard cups to within ¼ inch of top. Place cups in a pan of hot water; bake about 60 minutes, or until silver knife inserted near center comes out clean. Serve warm or chilled. Sprinkle with grated nutmeg, if desired.

Makes 5 servings, each 81 calories; 7 grams protein; 3.5 grams fat; 5 grams carbohydrate. (With sugar, 138 calories)

> *1 serving = ½ meat exchange*
> *½ cup skim milk*

Smooth as cream and deliciously sweet, these delicate custards are the kind of ambrosial dessert that dieters, and nondieters, dream about. Take your choice from vanilla, coffee, almond or chocolate.

Vanilla Pots de Crème

> 2 cups skim milk
> 1 tablespoon liquid *Sucaryl*
> 1 teaspoon vanilla
> 6 egg yolks

Preheat oven to 325°F. Scald milk; blend in *Sucaryl* and vanilla. Beat yolks until thick and lemon-colored; add milk, stirring constantly. Pour into 6 half-cup crème pots or small custard cups. Set pots in a pan of hot water; cover pan with foil and bake about 30 minutes, or until a knife inserted in the center comes out clean. Serve chilled.

Makes 6 servings, each 90 calories; 5.5 grams protein; 5.5 grams fat; 4 grams carbohydrate. (With sugar, 162 calories)

1 serving = ½ cup milk or ½ cup skim milk
+ 1 fat exchange

Coffee Pots de Crème

Prepare Vanilla Pots de Crème recipe, substituting 1 tablespoon instant coffee for the vanilla.

Nutritional analysis same as for Vanilla Pots de Crème.

Almond Pots de Crème

Prepare Vanilla Pots de Crème recipe, substituting ½ teaspoon almond extract for the vanilla.

Nutritional analysis same as for Vanilla Pots de Crème.

Chocolate Pots de Crème

Prepare Vanilla Pots de Crème recipe, adding 1 ounce unsweetened chocolate, grated, to the scalded milk; heat until chocolate melts.

Makes 6 servings, each 114 calories; 6 grams protein; 8 grams fat; 5.5 grams carbohydrate. (With sugar, 186 calories)

1 serving = ½ fat exchange
½ cup milk or ½ cup skim milk
+ 1 fat exchange

Baked Vanilla Soufflé

Light and ephemeral, the sweet dessert soufflé should qualify as one of the more inspired of all culinary creations. This *Sucaryl*-sweetened soufflé (and all those that follow) is just as delicately light and deliciously sweet as its high-calorie counterpart.

⅓ cup quick-cooking tapioca
1 cup skim milk
1 tablespoon liquid *Sucaryl*
¼ cup softened butter
2 tablespoons vanilla
6 eggs, separated

Preheat oven to 325°F. Tie a collar of waxed paper around edge of a lightly buttered 6-cup soufflé dish, letting collar extend 1½ inches above edge of dish. In saucepan, combine tapioca, milk and *Sucaryl*. Cook over medium heat, stirring constantly, until mixture comes to the full boil. Remove from heat; blend in softened butter and vanilla. Beat egg yolks with electric mixer until thick and lemon-colored; slowly add tapioca mixture. Beat egg whites until stiff but not dry. Fold into tapioca mixture. Carefully pour into prepared soufflé dish. With tip of spoon, circle top of soufflé about 1 inch in from side and about 1 inch deep. Set soufflé dish in pan of hot water. Bake 75 minutes. Serve immediately. For an extra flavor fillip, serve with Brandy Sauce, page 176.

Makes 6 servings, each 188 calories; 7.5 grams protein; 13 grams fat; 10 grams carbohydrate. (With sugar, 260 calories)

1 serving = ½ bread exchange
2 fat exchanges
1 meat exchange

Baked Chocolate Soufflé

¼ cup quick-cooking tapioca
1 cup skim milk
2 tablespoons liquid *Sucaryl*
2 ounces unsweetened chocolate, melted
¼ cup softened butter
1 teaspoon vanilla
6 eggs, separated

Preheat oven to 325°F. Tie a collar of waxed paper around edge of a lightly buttered 6-cup soufflé dish, letting collar extend 1½ inches above edge of dish. In saucepan, combine tapioca, milk and *Sucaryl*. Cook over medium heat, stirring constantly, until mixture comes to the full boil. Remove from heat; blend in melted chocolate, softened butter and vanilla. Beat egg yolks with electric mixer until thick and lemon-colored; slowly add tapioca mixture. Beat egg whites until stiff but not dry. Fold into tapioca mixture. Pour into prepared soufflé dish. With tip of spoon, circle top of soufflé about 1 inch in from side and about 1 inch deep. Set soufflé dish in a pan of hot water. Bake 75 minutes. Serve at once.

Makes 6 servings, each 228 calories; 8 grams protein; 18 grams fat; 10.5 grams carbohydrate. (With sugar, 372 calories)

> *1 serving = ½ bread exchange*
> *3 fat exchanges*
> *1 meat exchange*

Baked Apricot Soufflé

2 tablespoons butter
2 tablespoons flour
⅛ teaspoon salt
1 1-pound can low-calorie apricot halves, drained

1 tablespoon liquid *Sucaryl*
1 tablespoon apricot brandy
4 eggs, separated

Preheat oven to 325°F. Tie a collar of waxed paper around edge of a lightly buttered, 4-cup soufflé dish, letting collar extend 1½ inches above edge of dish. In saucepan, melt butter; blend in flour and salt. Purée apricots and blend into mixture in saucepan. Cook, stirring constantly, over medium heat until thickened. Add *Sucaryl* and brandy; gradually add to well-beaten egg yolks. Beat egg whites until stiff peaks form; gently fold into apricot mixture. Pour into prepared soufflé dish. Set in pan of hot water. Bake 60 minutes. Serve at once.

Makes 4 servings, each 193 calories; 7 grams protein; 11 grams fat; 13 grams carbohydrate. (With sugar, 301 calories)

> *1 serving = 1 fat exchange*
> *1½ fruit exchanges*
> *1 meat exchange*

Baked Brandy Soufflé

2 tablespoons butter
2 tablespoons flour
⅛ teaspoon salt
½ cup skim milk

1 tablespoon liquid *Sucaryl*
2 tablespoons brandy
5 eggs, separated

Preheat oven to 325°F. Tie a collar of waxed paper around edge of a lightly buttered 4-cup soufflé dish, letting collar stand 1½ inches above edge of dish. In saucepan, melt butter; blend in flour and salt; slowly add milk. Cook over medium heat, stirring constantly, until thickened. Add *Sucaryl* and brandy; gradually add to well-beaten egg yolks. Beat egg whites until stiff peaks form; gently fold into egg-yolk mixture. Pour into prepared soufflé dish. Set in pan of hot water. Bake 60 minutes. Serve at once.

Makes 4 servings, each 187 calories; 9 grams protein; 12.5 grams fat; 4.5 grams carbohydrate. (With sugar, 295 calories)

1 serving = 2 fat exchanges
1 meat exchange

Baked Orange Soufflé

¼ cup butter
5 tablespoons flour
¼ teaspoon salt
1 cup skim milk
3 tablespoons orange juice
1 tablespoon lemon juice
1 tablespoon grated orange rind
1 tablespoon liquid *Sucaryl*
4 eggs, separated
½ teaspoon vanilla
⅛ teaspoon almond extract

Preheat oven to 325°F. In saucepan, melt butter; blend in flour and salt. Add milk, orange and lemon juices, orange rind and *Sucaryl*; cook, stirring constantly, until thick. Slowly add to well-beaten egg yolks. Stir in vanilla and almond extract. Beat egg whites until stiff; fold into orange mixture. Pour into a lightly buttered 6-cup soufflé dish. Place dish in a pan of hot water; bake 60 minutes. Serve at once.

Makes 6 servings, each 157 calories; 6 grams protein; 11.5 grams fat; 7.5 grams carbohydrate. (With sugar, 229 calories)

1 serving = ½ bread exchange
1 fat exchange
1 meat exchange

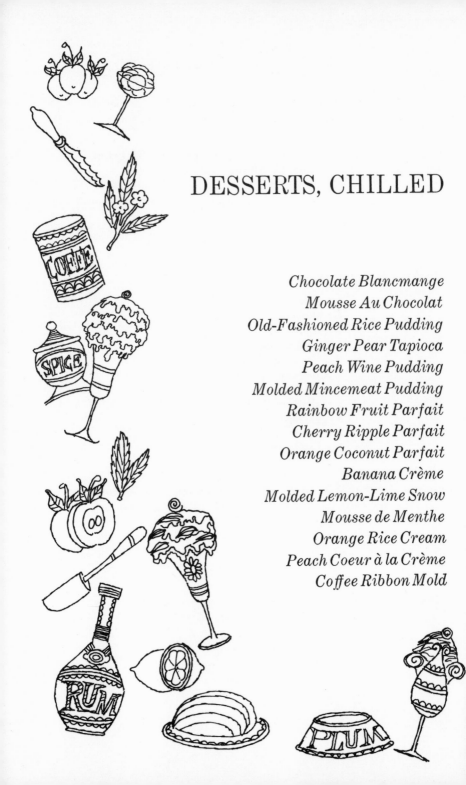

DESSERTS, CHILLED

Chocolate Blancmange
Mousse Au Chocolat
Old-Fashioned Rice Pudding
Ginger Pear Tapioca
Peach Wine Pudding
Molded Mincemeat Pudding
Rainbow Fruit Parfait
Cherry Ripple Parfait
Orange Coconut Parfait
Banana Crème
Molded Lemon-Lime Snow
Mousse de Menthe
Orange Rice Cream
Peach Coeur à la Crème
Coffee Ribbon Mold

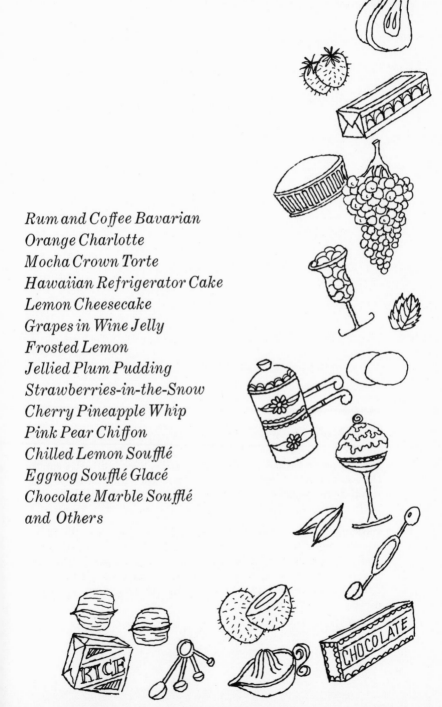

Rum and Coffee Bavarian
Orange Charlotte
Mocha Crown Torte
Hawaiian Refrigerator Cake
Lemon Cheesecake
Grapes in Wine Jelly
Frosted Lemon
Jellied Plum Pudding
Strawberries-in-the-Snow
Cherry Pineapple Whip
Pink Pear Chiffon
Chilled Lemon Soufflé
Eggnog Soufflé Glacé
Chocolate Marble Soufflé
and Others

Some changes have been made in blancmange since its heyday in Victorian times. This delicate snow-white pudding (its French name means "white food") still looks and tastes much the same, but modern calorie-saving recipes such as those featured here make it possible to enjoy this delightful dessert without fret about adding bulges to the waistline.

Basically, blancmange is a simple pudding made with milk, sweetening, a thickener, such as cornstarch, arrowroot or flour, and a flavoring. It may be served as an extravagantly shaped, quivering mold, or it may be served in simple dessert dishes. And it may depart from basic white to chocolate, coconut, mocha or fruit colors.

Vanilla Blancmange

> 2¼ cups skim milk
> 3 tablespoons cornstarch
> 2 teaspoons liquid *Sucaryl*
> ⅛ teaspoon salt
> 1½ teaspoons vanilla

In top of double boiler, blend ¼ cup of the milk into the cornstarch. Scald remaining 2 cups milk; gradually blend into cornstarch with *Sucaryl* and salt. Cook over boiling water, stirring constantly, until mixture thickens. Continue to cook, stirring occasionally, for 10 minutes to cook cornstarch completely. Remove from heat; blend in vanilla. Turn into individual molds or dessert dishes; refrigerate at least 1 hour before serving.

Makes 4 servings, each 70 calories; 5 grams protein; trace of fat; 12 grams carbohydrate. (With sugar, 142 calories)

> *1 serving = ½ bread exchange*
> *½ cup skim milk*

Coconut Blancmange

Prepare Vanilla Blancmange recipe, adding ½ cup dried shredded coconut to the milk before scalding. Reduce vanilla to ½ teaspoon and add ¼ teaspoon almond extract.

Makes 4 servings, each 113 calories; 5 grams protein; 3 grams fat; 16.5 grams carbohydrate. (With sugar, 185 calories)

> *1 serving = ½ bread exchange*
> *½ cup milk or ½ cup skim milk*
> *+ 1 fat exchange*

Mocha Blancmange

Prepare Chocolate Blancmange recipe, adding 2 teaspoons instant coffee to the cornstarch mixture.

Nutritional analysis same as for Chocolate Blancmange.

Chocolate Blancmange

Prepare Vanilla Blancmange recipe, blending 1 ounce melted unsweetened chocolate with the scalded milk. Increase the *Sucaryl* to 3 teaspoons and decrease vanilla to 1 teaspoon.

Makes 4 servings, each 106 calories; 5 grams protein; 4 grams fat; 14.5 grams carbohydrate. (With sugar, 214 calories)

> 1 serving = ½ bread exchange
> ½ cup milk or ½ cup skim milk
> + 1 fat exchange

English Custard (Stirred Custard Sauce)

A custard, properly prepared, is a delicate affair, its velvety smoothness pure pleasure to the palate. Nutritious, and easily digested, custards are considered especially good for children and invalids. At the same time, those with somewhat sophisticated tastes rate the custard a true delicacy.

Care should be taken in cooking custards in order to preserve their delicate flavor and insure a fine texture. Use of low heat is a cardinal rule. Too high a cooking temperature can cause the eggs to curdle or separate. Custards should be stirred constantly while cooking, and should not be permitted to boil at any time.

Chill this custard thoroughly, and serve as a pudding or as a sauce with fruits. (For a thicker custard filling, see Thick Custard Cream, page 180.)

3 cups skim milk	5 egg yolks
1 tablespoon liquid *Sucaryl*	1 teaspoon vanilla
2 tablespoons flour	

In top of double boiler, combine milk and *Sucaryl;* heat. Combine flour and egg yolks; beat well. Add a small amount of the hot milk to the egg mixture, blending well. Return mixture to top of double boiler. Cook over simmering water, stirring constantly, until mixture thickens slightly (about 15 minutes). Immediately remove from heat; pour into heatproof bowl and stir in flavoring. Place in refrigerator to chill rapidly. (Custard thickens more as it chills.)

Makes 3½ cups, each half-cup serving 88 calories; 6 grams protein; 4 grams fat; 7 grams carbohydrate. (With sugar, 150 calories)

1 serving = ½ cup milk or ½ cup skim milk
+ 1 fat exchange

Coffee Crème

If you're both a coffee lover and a calorie counter, you'll especially welcome this elegant dessert. In addition to calorie-free sweetening, a low-calorie powdered creamer is used to add richness of flavor and to help keep calories low.

1 cup nondairy powdered creamer
1 envelope unflavored gelatin
2 tablespoons instant coffee
Dash of salt

3 eggs, separated
1 tablespoon liquid *Sucaryl*
2 cups boiling water
1 teaspoon vanilla

In top of double boiler, combine creamer, gelatin, instant coffee and salt. Beat egg yolks and add to mixture with *Sucaryl* and boiling water. Cook over hot water, stirring constantly, until gelatin dissolves and mixture coats a silver spoon. Remove from heat; add vanilla; chill until mixture just begins to thicken. Beat egg whites until soft peaks form; fold into gelatin; chill until mixture mounds from spoon. Spoon into dessert dish. Garnish, if desired, with Low-Calorie Whipped Topping, page 178.

Makes 6 servings, each 132 calories; 5 grams protein; 9.5 grams fat; 9.5 grams carbohydrate. (With sugar and light cream, 279 calories)

1 serving = ½ bread exchange
1 fat exchange
1 meat exchange

Coffee Custard Pudding

This coffee-flavored pudding is somewhat less rich than the preceding Coffee Crème.

⅓ cup flour
2 tablespoons instant coffee
¼ teaspoon salt
2 cups skim milk, scalded
4½ teaspoons liquid *Sucaryl*
2 eggs, slightly beaten
1 teaspoon vanilla

In top of double boiler, combine flour, coffee and salt; slowly add scalded milk to make a smooth mixture. Add *Sucaryl* and eggs, blending well. Cook in top of double boiler, stirring constantly until thick, about 10 minutes. Remove from heat; cool; add vanilla. Pour into serving dish or individual dessert dishes, and chill. If desired, serve with mounds of Low-Calorie Whipped Topping, page 178.

Makes 5 servings, each 92 calories; 6.5 grams protein; 2.5 grams fat; 10.5 grams carbohydrate. (With sugar, 222 calories)

*1 serving = ½ meat exchange
½ cup skim milk*

Creamy Chocolate Pudding

5 tablespoons flour
⅓ cup cocoa
¼ teaspoon salt
3 cups skim milk
4½ teaspoons liquid *Sucaryl*
1 teaspoon vanilla

Combine flour, cocoa and salt in saucepan. Slowly add milk and

Combine milk, cinnamon and rice in top of double boiler. Cook over boiling water 45 minutes. Remove cinnamon; add raisins and cook 10 minutes longer. Remove from heat. Beat egg slightly with *Sucaryl*, salt and vanilla. Stir into rice. Return to double boiler and cook 2 minutes longer.

Makes 6 servings, each 108 calories; 6 grams protein; 1 gram fat; 19 grams carbohydrate. (With sugar, 180 calories)

> *1 serving = 1 bread exchange*
> *½ cup skim milk*

Lemon Rice Velvet

> 2 envelopes unflavored gelatin
> ½ cup lemon juice
> 2½ cups boiling water
> ¼ cup raw rice
> 2 tablespoons liquid *Sucaryl*
> ¼ cup nonfat dry milk
> ¼ cup ice water
> ¼ teaspoon almond extract

Soften gelatin in lemon juice; dissolve in 1½ cups boiling water. Combine rice and the remaining 1 cup boiling water; cook over low heat about 25 minutes, or until done. Place in electric blender with *Sucaryl* and dissolved gelatin; blend about 1 minute. Chill until mixture begins to thicken (about 2 hours). Then combine dry milk, ice water and almond extract; beat on high speed of mixer until of consistency of whipped cream. Fold into rice mixture. Spoon into sherbet glasses; chill until set.

Makes 6 servings, each 62 calories; 5.5 grams protein; trace of fat; 10.5 grams carbohydrate. (With sugar, 206 calories)

> *1 serving = ½ bread exchange*
> *¼ cup skim milk*

Amy Vanderbilt's Sugar-Free Zabaglione

4 egg yolks
4½ teaspoons liquid *Sucaryl*
2 teaspoons grated lemon rind
5 teaspoons lemon juice
¾ cup sherry wine

Use large glass or enamel double boiler. In lower pan heat enough water to almost touch bottom of top pan. Set top pan in place. Beat yolks slightly in it. Beat in remaining ingredients gradually. Continue to beat with rotary beater over boiling water until mixture is as thick and fluffy as whipped cream. Remove from water at once. Serve warm in parfait or sherbet glasses.

Makes 4 servings, each 125 calories; 3 grams protein; 5.5 grams fat; 4 grams carbohydrate. (With sugar, 287 calories)

Because of alcoholic content, consult physician before including in exchange-system diet.

Cranberry Apple Tapioca

2 cups raw cranberries
3 medium apples, pared, cored and sliced
3 tablespoons quick-cooking tapioca
½ teaspoon salt
2 cups water
7½ teaspoons liquid *Sucaryl*
1 teaspoon vanilla extract

Combine all ingredients in large saucepan. Cook over medium heat, stirring constantly, until mixture thickens. Reduce heat; continue to cook, stirring occasionally, until berries pop and apples are tender. Remove from heat. Serve warm or chilled.

Makes 6 servings, each 73 calories; 0.5 gram protein; 0.5 gram fat; 18 grams carbohydrate. (With sugar, 253 calories)

1 serving = ½ bread exchange
1 fruit exchange

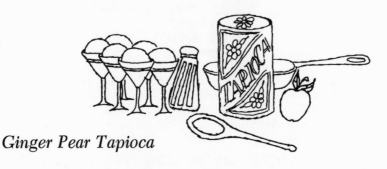

Ginger Pear Tapioca

2 cups water
4 teaspoons liquid *Sucaryl*
⅛ teaspoon salt
½ teaspoon ginger
2 pears, pared, cored and diced tapioca
3 tablespoons quick-cooking
2 maraschino cherries, chopped
2 tablespoons cherry juice
2 tablespoons lemon juice

Combine water, *Sucaryl*, salt and ginger. Add pears. Simmer until pears are tender. Strain, adding enough water to the liquid to make 2 cups. Add tapioca to liquid and cook over medium heat, stirring constantly, until thick. Remove from heat. Add pears and remaining ingredients. Cool, stirring occasionally. Spoon into sherbet glasses and chill.

Makes 6 servings, each 56 calories; 0.5 gram protein; trace of fat; 14 grams carbohydrate. (With sugar, 152 calories)

1 serving = ½ bread exchange
½ fruit exchange

Tapioca Pudding, White House Style

Lyndon Baines Johnson admits to a penchant for tapioca pudding sweetened this no-calorie way.

1 egg
2 teaspoons liquid *Sucaryl*
3 tablespoons quick-cooking tapioca
⅛ teaspoon salt
2¾ cups skim milk
1 teaspoon vanilla

Beat egg slightly; mix with *Sucaryl*, tapioca, salt and milk in saucepan; let stand 5 minutes. Cook over medium heat, stirring constantly, until mixture comes to the full boil and is thick. (Mixture thickens more upon cooling.) Remove from heat; add vanilla; cool.

Makes 4 servings, each 104 calories; 7.5 grams protein; 1.5 grams fat; 15 grams carbohydrate. (With sugar, 176 calories)

1 serving = ½ bread exchange
½ cup skim milk

Peach Wine Pudding

4 eggs, separated
2 tablespoons liquid *Sucaryl*
1 1-pound can low-calorie
    sliced peaches, drained and crushed
2 tablespoons lemon juice
½ cup white wine
1 envelope unflavored gelatin
½ cup cold water

Combine egg yolks and *Sucaryl*; beat on high speed of mixer until light and fluffy. Add peach pulp, lemon juice and wine. Cook in top of double boiler until smooth and thick. Soften gelatin in cold water; add to cooked mixture, stirring to dissolve. Allow to cool, stirring occasionally. When mixture has thickened, beat egg whites until peaks form; fold into gelatin mixture. Spoon into serving dish or sherbet glasses. Chill.

Makes 8 servings, each 79 calories; 4.5 grams protein; 2.5 grams fat; 5 grams carbohydrate. (With sugar, 187 calories)

1 serving = ½ fruit exchange
½ meat exchange

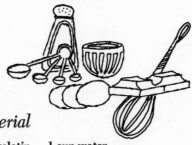

Molded Grape Imperial

2 envelopes unflavored gelatin	1 cup water
2 teaspoons grated orange rind	½ cup orange juice
½ teaspoon grated lemon rind	¼ cup lemon juice
¼ teaspoon salt	1 teaspoon vanilla
2 tablespoons liquid *Sucaryl*	2 cups green seedless grapes
5 eggs, separated	

In top of double boiler, combine gelatin, orange rind, lemon rind, salt and *Sucaryl*. Gradually blend in well-beaten egg yolks, water, orange juice and lemon juice. Cook over hot water until mixture thickens (about 12 to 15 minutes). Remove from heat; blend in vanilla; chill until mixture begins to mound from spoon. Beat egg whites until stiff peaks begin to form; fold into the chilled gelatin mixture along with the grapes. Gently spoon into a lightly oiled 6-cup mold; chill until set. To serve, unmold and, if desired, garnish with additional grapes.

Makes 8 servings, each 91 calories; 6.5 grams protein; 3.5 grams fat; 9 grams carbohydrate. (With sugar, 199 calories)

1 serving = 1 fruit exchange
½ meat exchange

Molded Mincemeat Pudding

All sweetness and light, this airy holiday confection consists of rich-flavored mincemeat, blended to cloudlike softness with gelatin and fluffy egg whites.

1½ tablespoons unflavored gelatin
¼ cup cold water
3 eggs, separated
2 tablespoons liquid *Sucaryl*
1¾ cups orange juice
½ teaspoon salt
1 teaspoon grated orange rind
⅛ teaspoon cinnamon
1 cup mincemeat

Soften gelatin in cold water. In top of double boiler, combine egg yolks, *Sucaryl*, orange juice, salt, orange rind and cinnamon. Cook over hot water, stirring constantly, until slightly thickened. Remove from heat; add softened gelatin, stirring to dissolve gelatin. Chill until mixture begins to thicken slightly; fold in mincemeat. Beat egg whites until stiff peaks form; fold into gelatin mixture. Spoon into a slightly oiled 5-cup mold; chill until set.

Makes 6 servings, each 195 calories; 8.5 grams protein; 6.5 grams fat; 26.5 grams carbohydrate. (With sugar, 339 calories)

1 serving = 1 bread exchange
1 fruit exchange
1 meat exchange

Crème de Menthe Parfait

This ethereal invention consists of alternating layers of sparkling, minted lime gelatin and low-calorie whipped topping, deliciously flavored with crème de menthe and crème de cacao.

2 envelopes unflavored gelatin
½ cup cold water
1½ cups boiling water
1½ cups lime juice
3 tablespoons liquid *Sucaryl*
1 tablespoon green crème de menthe
¼ cup nonfat dry milk
¼ cup ice water
1 tablespoon crème de cacao

Soften gelatin in cold water; add boiling water, stirring to dissolve. Add lime juice, *Sucaryl* and crème de menthe. Chill until firm; then force gelatin through sieve. Combine dry milk and ice water; beat on high speed of mixer until of consistency of whipped cream. Blend in crème de cacao. To serve, alternate layers of minted lime gelatin and whipped milk in 6 parfait glasses.

Makes 6 servings, each 58 calories; 5 grams protein; trace of fat; 9 grams carbohydrate. (With sugar, 274 calories)

*1 serving = ½ fruit exchange
½ cup skim milk*

Rainbow Fruit Parfait

6½ teaspoons liquid *Sucaryl*	3 tablespoons quick-cooking
1 cup fresh strawberries, sliced	tapioca
1 cup sliced fresh peaches	⅛ teaspoon salt
1 cup fresh blueberries	2¾ cups skim milk
1 egg, slightly beaten	1 teaspoon vanilla

Combine 1½ teaspoons of the *Sucaryl* with each cup of fruit. Refrigerate until ready to use. Combine beaten egg, remaining 2 teaspoons *Sucaryl*, tapioca, salt and milk in saucepan; let stand 5 minutes. Cook over medium heat, stirring constantly, until mixture comes to the full boil and is thick (mixture thickens more upon cooling). Remove from heat; add vanilla; cool. Alternate layers of tapioca and fruits in parfait glasses. Serve chilled.

Makes 6 servings, each 105 calories; 5.5 grams protein; 1.5 grams fat; 19 grams carbohydrates. (With sugar, 261 calories)

*1 serving = 1½ fruit exchanges
½ cup skim milk*

Apricot Tapioca Parfait

⅓ cup quick-cooking tapioca
2 tablespoons liquid *Sucaryl*
¼ teaspoon salt
2 1-pint cans low-calorie
  apricot nectar
¼ cup nonfat dry milk
¼ cup ice water

Combine tapioca, *Sucaryl*, salt and apricot nectar in saucepan. Cook over medium heat, stirring constantly, until mixture comes to the full boil and thickens. Divide 3 cups of this mixture among 6 parfait or sherbet glasses. Chill remaining 1 cup of mixture. Combine dry milk and ice water; beat on high speed of mixer until of consistency of whipped cream. Fold in the chilled apricot mixture. Spoon on top of plain apricot tapioca.

Makes 6 servings, each 85 calories; 2 grams protein; trace of fat; 18.5 grams carbohydrate. (With sugar, 229 calories)

1 serving = ½ bread exchange
1 fruit exchange

Coffee Banana Parfait

½ cup nondairy powdered
  creamer
6 tablespoons flour
¼ teaspoon salt
1 tablespoon liquid *Sucaryl*
2 eggs, slightly beaten
2 cups strong, hot coffee
1 tablespoon butter
½ teaspoon vanilla
3 medium bananas, sliced

In top of double boiler, combine powdered creamer, flour, salt, *Sucaryl* and eggs. Gradually add hot coffee, stirring to blend. Cook over hot water, stirring constantly, until mixture is thick and smooth. Remove from heat; blend in butter and vanilla. Chill until mixture sets. Alternate layers of coffee pudding and sliced bananas in parfait glasses.

Makes 6 servings, each 155 calories; 3.5 grams protein; 7.5 grams fat; 21.5 grams carbohydrate. (With sugar and light cream, 265 calories)

> 1 serving = 1 bread exchange
> 1 fat exchange
> 1 fruit exchange

Applesauce Custard Parfait

Spiced Applesauce	*Custard*
2 pounds apples	1 tablespoon cornstarch
½ cup water	¼ teaspoon salt
1 tablespoon liquid *Sucaryl*	3 eggs, well beaten
1 tablespoon lemon juice	2 teaspoons liquid *Sucaryl*
1 teaspoon cinnamon	2 cups skim milk

Pare, core and quarter apples; place in saucepan with water. Cover and simmer 15 to 20 minutes, or until tender. Mash with a fork, or force through food mill. Add the 1 tablespoon *Sucaryl*, lemon juice and cinnamon; chill several hours to allow cinnamon to flavor applesauce.

In saucepan, combine cornstarch and salt. Blend in eggs, the 2 teaspoons *Sucaryl* and milk; cook over medium heat, stirring constantly, until mixture comes to the boil and thickens. Remove from heat and chill well.

Alternate layers of spiced applesauce and custard in parfait glasses.

Makes 6 servings, each 150 calories; 6.5 grams protein; 3.5 grams fat; 25.5 grams carbohydrate. (With sugar, 270 calories)

> 1 serving = 2 fruit exchanges
> ½ meat exchange
> ½ cup skim milk

Cherry Ripple Parfait

Custard	**Cherry Sauce**
1½ teaspoons cornstarch	1 1-pound can water-pack red
⅛ teaspoon salt	sour cherries
2 eggs, well beaten	1 tablespoon cornstarch
1 teaspoon liquid *Sucaryl*	1 tablespoon liquid *Sucaryl*
1 cup skim milk	Red food coloring
¼ teaspoon vanilla	

Combine all custard ingredients except vanilla in small saucepan. Cook over medium heat, stirring constantly, until thick and smooth. Remove from heat; add vanilla and chill until set.

Drain cherries; measure liquid and add enough water to make 1 cup. Gradually add liquid to cornstarch in saucepan, stirring until smooth. Add *Sucaryl* and cook over medium heat, stirring constantly, until thick and clear. Remove from heat; add cherries and food coloring, as desired. Chill until almost set.

Carefully fold cherry sauce into custard to give a rippled effect. Serve in parfait glasses or a large glass bowl.

Makes 4 servings, each 125 calories; 6 grams protein; 3 grams fat; 19.5 grams carbohydrate. (With sugar, 270 calories)

1 serving = 1½ fruit exchanges
½ meat exchange
¼ cup skim milk

Blueberry Coconut Parfait

⅓ cup flour	2½ cups skim milk, scalded
¼ teaspoon salt	1 teaspoon vanilla
2 eggs, well beaten	½ cup dried shredded coconut
2½ tablespoons liquid *Sucaryl*	2 cups blueberries

Combine flour and salt in top of double boiler; add eggs and 1½ tablespoons *Sucaryl*, stirring until smooth. Gradually add the scalded milk; cook over medium heat, stirring constantly until thick. Remove from heat; cool and add vanilla and coconut.

Sweeten blueberries with the remaining 1 tablespoon *Sucaryl*. Alternate layers of pudding and sweetened blueberries in parfait glasses. Chill before serving.

Makes 6 servings, each 141 calories; 6.5 grams protein; 4 grams fat; 19.5 grams carbohydrate. (With sugar, 321 calories)

> *1 serving = ½ bread exchange*
> *½ fruit exchange*
> *½ cup milk or ½ cup skim milk*
> *+ 1 fat exchange*

Orange Coconut Parfait

> 2 tablespoons cornstarch
> 1½ tablespoons unflavored gelatin
> ¼ teaspoon salt
> 2½ cups skim milk
> 2 tablespoons liquid *Sucaryl*
> 2 teaspoons vanilla extract
> ¼ teaspoon almond extract
> ½ cup dried shredded coconut
> 3 egg whites
> 2 10½-ounce cans low-calorie
> mandarin oranges

In top of double boiler, combine cornstarch, gelatin, salt, milk and *Sucaryl*. Cook over boiling water, stirring constantly, until thickened. Remove from heat; add vanilla and almond extracts. Chill until mixture begins to mound from spoon; blend in coconut. Beat egg whites until soft peaks form; fold into gelatin mixture. Drain orange sections and alternate gelatin mixture with oranges in parfait glasses. Chill.

Makes 6 servings, each 116 calories; 8 grams protein; 2 grams fat; 16 grams carbohydrate. (With sugar, 260 calories)

> *1 serving = 1 fruit exchange*
> *½ meat exchange*
> *½ cup skim milk*

All of the molded dessert creams and Bavarians which follow taste devastatingly rich and creamy, yet boast of a minimum of calories. In addition to the use of calorie-free sweetening in place of sugar, a nondairy powdered creamer and nonfat dry milk are frequently used to provide low-calorie replacements for cream.

Spanish Cream

1½ tablespoons unflavored gelatin	3 eggs, separated
½ cup cold water	3 cups hot water
1½ cups nondairy powdered creamer	4½ teaspoons liquid *Sucaryl*
	1 tablespoon vanilla

Soften gelatin in cold water. In top of double boiler, combine powdered creamer, egg yolks, water and *Sucaryl*. Cook, stirring constantly, over simmering water, only until mixture coats spoon (about 8 to 10 minutes). Remove from heat; add softened gelatin and vanilla, stirring to dissolve gelatin. Refrigerate until mixture begins to thicken. Beat egg whites until stiff peaks form; fold into custard. Spoon into a lightly oiled 6-cup mold; chill until set. Unmold to serve.

Makes 8 servings, each 134 calories; 5.0 grams protein; 10 grams fat; 11 grams carbohydrate. (With sugar, 215 calories)

> *1 serving = 1 bread exchange*
> *1 fat exchange*
> *½ meat exchange*

Banana Crème

2 envelopes unflavored gelatin	¼ cup sherry
1¼ cups water	4 medium bananas, mashed
1 cup orange juice	⅓ cup nonfat dry milk
2 tablespoons liquid *Sucaryl*	⅓ cup ice water
1 tablespoon lemon juice	

Soften gelatin in ¼ cup of the water. Bring remaining 1 cup water to the boil; add to gelatin, stirring to dissolve. Add orange juice, *Sucaryl*, lemon juice and sherry. Blend in mashed bananas. Chill until mixture begins to set. Combine dry milk and ice water; beat on high speed of mixer until peaks form. Fold into gelatin. Spoon into a lightly oiled 6-cup mold. Chill until set.

Makes 8 servings, each 95 calories; 5 grams protein; trace of fat; 18 grams carbohydrate. (With sugar, 203 calories)

1 serving = 1½ fruit exchanges
¼ cup skim milk

Citrus Crème

1 6-ounce can frozen unsweet-ened orange-pineapple juice concentrate	4½ teaspoons liquid *Sucaryl*
2 envelopes unflavored gelatin	2 tablespoons orange curaçao
½ cup cold water	½ cup nonfat dry milk
	½ cup ice water

Reconstitute juice concentrate as directed. Bring juice to the boil; heat for 2 minutes. (If juice is not heated, the enzymes in the pineapple juice will prevent the mixture from forming a gel.) In a large mixer bowl, soften gelatin in cold water. Add the hot juice, *Sucaryl* and curaçao, stirring to dissolve the gela-tin. Chill until mixture becomes thick and syrupy. Combine dry milk and ice water; beat on high speed of mixer until mix-ture holds its shape. Fold into gelatin; spoon into a lightly oiled 7-cup mold; chill until set.

Makes 9 servings, each 74 calories; 4.5 grams protein; trace of fat; 13 grams carbohydrate. (With sugar, 146 calories)

1 serving = ½ fruit exchange
½ cup skim milk

Peach Coconut Cream

 1 envelope unflavored gelatin
 ¼ cup cold water
 1 1-pound can low-calorie
   peach halves
 ⅓ cup cold water
 1 tablespoon liquid *Sucaryl*
 1 tablespoon lemon juice
 ¼ teaspoon almond extract
 ¼ cup nonfat dry milk
 ¼ cup ice water
 ⅓ cup dried shredded coconut

Soften gelatin in ¼ cup water; dissolve over boiling water. Purée peaches; add the dissolved gelatin, the ⅓ cup water, *Sucaryl*, lemon juice and almond extract; blend well. Chill until mixture begins to thicken. Combine dry milk and ice water; beat on high speed of mixer until soft peaks form. Fold the whipped milk and shredded coconut into the gelatin. Spoon into a lightly oiled 3-cup mold; chill until firm. If desired, garnish with additional peach slices and coconut.

Makes 5 servings, each 76 calories; 4.5 grams protein; 1.5 gram fat; 11.5 grams carbohydrate. (With sugar, 163 calories)

1 serving = ½ fruit exchange
½ cup skim milk

Molded Lemon-Lime Snow

This mint-green bit of froufrou is a dream of a dessert for dieters (or for anyone looking for a refreshingly cool, delectably sweet summer dessert).

> 2 envelopes unflavored gelatin
> ¼ cup cold water
> 1½ cups boiling water
> ¼ cup lemon juice
> ¼ cup lime juice
> 5 teaspoons liquid *Sucaryl*
> Few drops of green food coloring
> ⅓ cup nonfat dry milk
> ⅓ cup ice water

Soften gelatin in cold water; add boiling water to dissolve gelatin. Add lemon juice, lime juice and *Sucaryl;* chill until mixture becomes thick and syrupy. Add food coloring as desired. Combine dry milk and ice water in small bowl of mixer; beat on high speed until of consistency of whipped cream. Fold into gelatin. Spoon into a lightly oiled 4-cup mold; chill until set.

Makes 6 servings, each 40 calories; 5.5 grams protein; no fat; 5 grams carbohydrate. (With sugar, 160 calories)

1 serving = ½ cup skim milk

Mousse de Menthe

> 2 envelopes unflavored gelatin
> ½ cup lemon juice
> 2½ cups boiling water
> 4 teaspoons liquid *Sucaryl*
>
> 3 tablespoons crème de menthe
> ¼ cup nonfat dry milk
> ¼ cup ice water

Soften gelatin in lemon juice; dissolve in boiling water. Add *Sucaryl* and crème de menthe; chill until thickened. Combine dry milk and ice water; beat on high speed of mixer until of consistency of whipped cream. Fold into gelatin. Pour into a lightly oiled 4-cup mold; chill until set. Garnish with strawberries, if desired.

Makes 6 servings, each 59 calories; 5 grams protein; no fat; 6.5 grams carbohydrate. (With sugar, 155 calories)

1 serving = ½ cup skim milk

Orange Rice Cream

⅔ cup raw rice
1 quart skim milk
½ teaspoon salt
4½ teaspoons liquid *Sucaryl*
2 envelopes unflavored gelatin
½ cup orange juice
1 tablespoon grated orange rind
1 teaspoon vanilla
¼ cup nonfat dry milk
¼ cup ice water

Combine rice with milk, salt and *Sucaryl* in a saucepan. Bring
to the boil; reduce heat and cook over low heat about 30 minutes, or until rice is very soft. Force through a sieve. Soften
gelatin in orange juice. Add with the rind and vanilla to rice
mixture, blending well; cool 30 minutes. Combine dry milk and
ice water; beat on high speed of mixer until of consistency of
whipped cream. Fold into rice mixture. Spoon into a lightly
oiled 4-cup mold. Chill until set.

Makes 6 servings, each 173 calories; 12 grams protein; 0.5 gram
fat; 30 grams carbohydrate. (With sugar, 281 calories)

1 serving = 1 bread exchange
1 cup skim milk

Peach Coeur à la Crème

Traditionally made in a heart-shaped mold, this calorie-streamlined version of Coeur à la Crème is sheer bliss to eat.

2 envelopes unflavored gelatin
⅓ cup cold water
1 pound skim-milk cottage cheese
2 cups skim milk
2 tablespoons liquid *Sucaryl*
1 pound fresh ripe peaches

Soften gelatin in cold water; dissolve over boiling water. Force
cottage cheese through food mill until smooth. Add milk and

Sucaryl to cheese, blending until smooth. Add dissolved gelatin. Put peaches through food mill to make a purée; add to cheese mixture. Pour into a lightly oiled 6-cup heart-shaped mold; chill until set. To serve, unmold and garnish, if desired, with additional sweetened sliced peaches.

Makes 8 servings, each 107 calories; 15.5 grams protein; 0.5 gram fat; 10 grams carbohydrate. (With sugar, 215 calories)

> *1 serving = ½ fruit exchange*
> *1 meat exchange*
> *½ cup skim milk*

Molded Cinnamon Cream

Made with sour cream, this dessert tastes marvelously rich . . . yet contains relatively few calories.

> **2 envelopes unflavored gelatin**
> **¼ cup cold water**
> **3 cups skim milk**
> **2 tablespoons liquid *Sucaryl***
> **3 sticks cinnamon**
> **1 cup sour cream**
> **1 teaspoon vanilla**

Soften gelatin in cold water. Combine milk, *Sucaryl* and cinnamon sticks in saucepan; heat for 10 to 15 minutes; remove cinnamon. Add the hot milk to the softened gelatin, stirring to dissolve. Chill until mixture begins to thicken. Combine sour cream and vanilla, beating until smooth. Fold into gelatin mixture. Turn into a lightly oiled 4-cup mold. Chill until firm. Serve with garnish of fresh fruit, if desired.

Makes 6 servings, each 135 calories; 8.5 grams protein; 8 grams fat; 7.5 grams carbohydrate. (With sugar, 279 calories)

> *1 serving = 1 fat exchange*
> *½ cup milk or ½ cup skim milk*
> *+ 1 fat exchange*

Coffee Ribbon Mold

When you turn this unusual coffee-flavored confection out of its mold, you'll find that three distinct layers or ribbons have formed. On the bottom is a coffee custard, in the middle a coffee jelly, on top a coffee sponge or soufflé. Looks lovely, tastes even better.

> 3 envelopes unflavored gelatin
> ¼ cup cold water
> 2 cups hot skim milk
> 3 eggs, separated
> ⅛ teaspoon salt
> 2 cups strong coffee
> 2 tablespoons liquid *Sucaryl*
> 1¼ teaspoons vanilla

Soften gelatin in cold water. Add hot milk slowly to beaten egg yolks in top of double boiler; add salt and coffee and cook for 5 minutes. Remove from heat and stir in gelatin until dissolved. Let cool slightly. Meanwhile, beat egg whites until foamy; add *Sucaryl* and beat until stiff peaks form; then add vanilla. Fold into custard mixture and pour into a lightly oiled 8-cup mold. Chill until firm.

Makes 12 servings, each 42 calories; 5 grams protein; 1.5 grams fat; 2 grams carbohydrate. (With sugar, 114 calories)

1 serving = ½ meat exchange

Molded Blueberry Cream

> 1 envelope unflavored gelatin
> ¼ cup cold water
> 2 cups buttermilk
> 2 tablespoons cornstarch
>
> 2 eggs, separated
> 1 tablespoon liquid *Sucaryl*
> ½ teaspoon almond extract
> 1 cup fresh blueberries

Soften gelatin in cold water; set aside. In top of double boiler, add a small amount of the buttermilk to cornstarch to make a smooth paste. Stir in remaining buttermilk and cook over medium heat, stirring until slightly thickened. Beat egg yolks until light and foamy; add a small amount of the hot liquid; then stir egg yolk mixture into hot liquid in double boiler and cook 5 minutes longer. Remove from heat; add softened gelatin, stirring to dissolve. Chill until mixture begins to thicken. Combine egg whites, *Sucaryl* and almond extract; beat until stiff peaks form; fold into gelatin mixture. Fold in blueberries. Spoon into a lightly oiled 4-cup mold; chill until set.

Makes 6 servings, each 84 calories; 6.5 grams protein; 2 grams fat; 10 grams carbohydrate. (With sugar, 156 calories)

> *1 serving = ½ fruit exchange*
> *½ cup skim milk*

Cherry Sherry Valentine

> 1 envelope unflavored gelatin
> ¼ cup sherry
> 1 1-pound can water-pack sour
>   red cherries
> 1 tablespoon lemon juice
> 1 tablespoon liquid *Sucaryl*
> ½ cup nonfat dry milk
> ½ cup ice water

Soften gelatin in sherry; dissolve over hot water. Add to cherries, lemon juice and *Sucaryl;* chill until mixture begins to thicken. Combine dry milk and ice water; beat on high speed of mixer until of consistency of whipped cream. Fold into gelatin mixture. Spoon into a lightly oiled 6-cup, heart-shaped mold. Chill until firm.

Makes 8 servings, each 69 calories; 4 grams protein; trace of fat; 11.5 grams carbohydrate. (With sugar, 123 calories)

> *1 serving = ½ fruit exchange*
> *½ cup skim milk*

Cherry Pecan Molded Cream

This festive dessert is scented with rum and studded with maraschino cherries and chopped pecans.

1 envelope unflavored gelatin
¼ cup skim milk
2 tablespoons rum
1½ cups skim milk, scalded
3 eggs, separated
4 teaspoons liquid *Sucaryl*
⅛ teaspoon salt
10 maraschino cherries, chopped
3 tablespoons chopped pecans

Soften gelatin in the ¼ cup milk and rum. Combine scalded milk, egg yolks, *Sucaryl* and salt in top of double boiler. Cook over hot water, stirring constantly, until slightly thickened. Remove from heat; add softened gelatin, stirring until gelatin dissolves. Chill until mixture begins to thicken. Fold in stiffly beaten egg whites, cherries and pecans. Turn into a lightly oiled 4-cup mold. Chill until set.

Makes 6 servings, each 139 calories; 7.5 grams protein; 5.5 grams fat; 13 grams carbohydrate. (With sugar, 235 calories)

1 serving = ½ fruit exchange
½ meat exchange
½ cup milk or ½ cup skim milk
+ 1 fat exchange

Norwegian Rum Pudding with Grape Sauce

Sweeten this delicious rum-flavored holiday pudding with *Sucaryl*, and save 216 calories in every serving.

2 envelopes unflavored gelatin
1½ cups water
6 egg yolks
2 tablespoons liquid *Sucaryl*
¼ cup rum
¾ cup nonfat dry milk
¾ cup ice water

Grape Sauce
1 tablespoon cornstarch
½ cup water
2 tablespoons liquid *Sucaryl*
1 cup unsweetened grape juice
2 tablespoons lemon juice

Soften gelatin in ¼ cup of the water. In top of double boiler, combine yolks, *Sucaryl* and remaining 1¼ cups water; beat until thick and lemon-colored. Place over hot water and cook, stirring constantly, until custard coats a spoon. Add rum and softened gelatin, stirring to dissolve gelatin. Refrigerate until mixture begins to thicken. Combine dry milk and ice water; beat on high speed of mixer until of consistency of whipped cream; fold into gelatin mixture. Spoon into a lightly oiled 6-cup mold; chill until set.

Combine all sauce ingredients in a saucepan. Cook over medium heat, stirring constantly, until slightly thickened and clear.

Chill and serve over pudding.

Makes 8 servings, each 138 calories; 8.5 grams protein; 4 grams fat; 13 grams carbohydrate. (With sugar, 354 calories)

1 serving = ½ fruit exchange
½ meat exchange
½ cup skim milk

No-Cook Lemon Bavarian Cream

2 envelopes unflavored gelatin
¼ cup cold water
1 cup boiling water
4 eggs, separated
½ cup nondairy powdered creamer
1½ tablespoons liquid *Sucaryl*
1 tablespoon grated lemon rind
⅓ cup lemon juice

Soften gelatin in cold water; dissolve in boiling water. Beat egg yolks; add powdered creamer, *Sucaryl*, lemon rind and juice. Blend in dissolved gelatin. Chill until slightly thickened; then whip until foamy. Beat egg whites until stiff; fold into gelatin. Spoon into a lightly oiled 6-cup mold; chill until set.

Makes 8 servings, each 82 calories; 5.5 grams protein; 5.5 grams fat; 4.5 grams carbohydrate. (With sugar, 163 calories)

1 serving = ½ bread exchange
½ meat exchange

Rhubarb Strawberry Bavarian

Rhubarb teams with strawberries in this temptingly sweet springtime party dessert. (Note that calories have been trimmed to one-fifth the usual count!)

2 cups rhubarb, cut into 1-inch pieces
¼ cup water
3 tablespoons liquid *Sucaryl*
2 envelopes unflavored gelatin
½ cup cold water
2 cups strawberries, crushed
¼ cup nonfat dry milk
¼ cup ice water

Combine rhubarb, ¼ cup water and *Sucaryl* in small saucepan.

Cover and simmer until fruit is well cooked. Soften gelatin in ½ cup water; add the hot cooked rhubarb, stirring to dissolve gelatin. Add strawberries; chill until mixture begins to set. Combine dry milk and ice water; beat on high speed of mixer until of consistency of whipped cream. Fold into thickened gelatin. Spoon into a lightly oiled 6-cup mold. Chill until set.

Makes 8 servings, each 40 calories; 4 grams protein; trace of fat; 6 grams carbohydrate. (With sugar, 202 calories)

> *1 serving = ½ fruit exchange*
> *¼ cup skim milk*

Rum and Coffee Bavarian

½ cup nondairy powdered creamer
2 tablespoons instant coffee
2 envelopes unflavored gelatin
½ teaspoon salt
4 eggs, separated

2 tablespoons liquid *Sucaryl*
2 cups boiling water
2 tablespoons rum
½ cup nonfat dry milk
½ cup ice water

In top of double boiler, combine powdered creamer, instant coffee, gelatin and salt. Beat egg yolks and add to mixture with *Sucaryl* and boiling water. Cook over hot water, stirring constantly, until gelatin dissolves and mixture becomes thick and smooth. Remove from heat; add rum; chill until mixture begins to set. Beat egg whites until soft peaks form; fold into gelatin mixture. Combine dry milk and ice water; beat on high speed of mixer until soft peaks form; fold into gelatin. Spoon into a lightly oiled 8-cup mold; chill until set.

Makes 12 servings, each 77 calories; 5.5 grams protein; 3.5 grams fat; 5 grams carbohydrate. (With sugar and light cream, 168 calories)

> *1 serving = ½ bread exchange*
> *½ meat exchange*

Orange Charlotte

2 envelopes unflavored gelatin	1½ cups orange sections, cut up
2 cups orange juice	⅓ cup nonfat dry milk
1½ cups boiling water	⅓ cup ice water
4 teaspoons liquid *Sucaryl*	6 small ladyfingers, split

Soften gelatin in ½ cup of the orange juice; add boiling water, stirring to dissolve. Add *Sucaryl* and remaining orange juice; chill until mixture begins to thicken; fold in cut-up orange sections. Combine dry milk and ice water; beat on high speed of mixer until peaks form. Fold into gelatin mixture. Line a 4-cup mold with split ladyfingers, rounded side out. Pour in orange filling. Chill until set. Unmold and garnish with orange slices and mint, as desired.

Makes 6 servings, each 115 calories; 7 grams protein; 0.5 gram fat; 22 grams carbohydrate. (With sugar, 211 calories)

1 serving = ½ bread exchange
1 fruit exchange
½ cup skim milk

Pineapple Charlotte

2 envelopes unflavored gelatin
¼ cup cold water
1½ cups unsweetened pine-
  apple juice
2 tablespoons liquid *Sucaryl*
⅛ teaspoon salt
2 tablespoons lemon juice
3 egg whites, stiffly beaten
½ cup nonfat dry milk
½ cup ice water
12 small ladyfingers, split

Soften gelatin in cold water. Heat pineapple juice; add to softened gelatin, stirring to dissolve. Add *Sucaryl*, salt and lemon juice. Refrigerate until thickened. Beat egg whites until stiff peaks form; fold into gelatin mixture. Combine dry milk and ice water; beat on high speed of mixer until of consistency of whipped cream. Fold into gelatin mixture. Line sides of a loaf pan (9 × 5 × 3 inches) with ladyfingers, rounded side out; add gelatin mixture and chill until set.

Makes 12 servings, each 65 calories; 4.5 grams protein; 0.5 gram fat; 11 grams carbohydrate. (With sugar, 137 calories)

1 serving = ½ bread exchange
½ fruit exchange

Strawberry Charlotte

3 envelopes unflavored gelatin	1½ tablespoons lemon juice
¾ cup cold water	¼ teaspoon salt
5 eggs, separated	⅓ cup nonfat dry milk
3 tablespoons liquid *Sucaryl*	⅓ cup ice water
5 cups fresh, hulled strawberries, crushed	12 small ladyfingers, split

Soften gelatin in cold water. In top of double boiler, combine egg yolks, *Sucaryl*, crushed strawberries, lemon juice and salt. Cook over hot water until mixture begins to thicken. Remove from heat; blend in softened gelatin, stirring to dissolve. Chill until mixture begins to thicken. Beat egg whites until stiff peaks form; fold into gelatin mixture. Combine dry milk and ice water; beat on high speed of mixer until of consistency of whipped cream; fold into gelatin. Line sides of a 10-cup mold with the split ladyfingers; spoon gelatin mixture into mold and chill until set.

Makes 12 servings, each 97 calories; 7 grams protein; 3 grams fat; 11.5 grams carbohydrate. (With sugar, 205 calories)

1 serving = ½ bread exchange
½ fruit exchange
1 meat exchange

Chocolate Charlotte

1 envelope unflavored gelatin	4 eggs, separated
1 tablespoon liquid *Sucaryl*	1 teaspoon vanilla
Dash of salt	¼ cup ice water
⅓ cup water	¼ cup nonfat dry milk
2 squares unsweetened chocolate	6 small ladyfingers, split

Combine gelatin, *Sucaryl*, salt, water and chocolate in top of double boiler. Cook over hot water until gelatin dissolves and chocolate is melted. Remove from heat; add egg yolks, one at a time, beating well after each addition. Return to top of double boiler and cook for 2 minutes. (Mixture will become very thick and cling in a ball in center of pan.) Remove from heat; add vanilla. Chill in refrigerator for 15 minutes. Meanwhile, combine egg whites, ice water and dry milk; beat on high speed of mixer until mixture is of consistency of whipped cream. Carefully fold into the cooled chocolate mixture. Place ladyfingers, rounded side out, around edge of loaf pan (7 × 3 × 2 inches). Carefully pour chocolate mixture into pan; chill until firm.

Makes 6 servings, each 141 calories; 8. 5 grams protein; 9 grams fat; 8.5 grams carbohydrate. (With sugar, 213 calories)

> *1 serving = ½ bread exchange*
> *1 fat exchange*
> *1 meat exchange*

Apricot Trifle Torte

3 envelopes unflavored gelatin	½ cup sherry
¼ teaspoon salt	1 1-pound can low-calorie apri-
3 tablespoons liquid *Sucaryl*	cot halves
8 eggs, separated	12 small ladyfingers, split
3 cups skim milk	

In top of double boiler, combine gelatin, salt, *Sucaryl* and egg yolks; blend well. Gradually blend in skim milk; cook over hot water, stirring constantly, until gelatin dissolves and mixture thickens slightly. Remove from heat; stir in sherry and liquid drained from apricots; chill until mixture begins to mound from spoon. Beat egg whites until soft peaks form; fold into gelatin mixture. Line sides of a 9-inch spring-form pan with ladyfingers, rounded side out. Carefully pour the gelatin mixture into the pan; chill until set. Arrange apricot halves on top, and if desired, garnish with Low-Calorie Whipped Topping, page 178.

Makes 12 servings, each 127 calories; 9 grams protein; 4 grams fat; 10 grams carbohydrate. (With sugar, 235 calories)

> *1 serving = ½ bread exchange*
> *½ fruit exchange*
> *1 meat exchange*

Mocha Crown Torte

4 envelopes unflavored gelatin	4 tablespoons liquid *Sucaryl*
⅔ cup cold water	¾ cup nonfat dry milk
¼ cup instant coffee	¾ cup ice water
1 tablespoon cocoa	12 small ladyfingers, split
1 quart skim milk	¼ cup almonds, chopped
8 eggs, separated	

Soften gelatin in cold water. In top of double boiler, combine instant coffee and cocoa. Add milk gradually, then egg yolks and *Sucaryl*. Cook over hot (not boiling) water, stirring constantly, until mixture coats spoon. Remove from heat; add softened gelatin, stirring until gelatin dissolves. Chill until mixture begins to thicken. Beat egg whites until stiff peaks begin to form; fold into gelatin mixture. Combine dry milk and ice water; beat on high speed of mixer until soft peaks form; fold into gelatin. Line sides of a 9-inch spring-form pan with ladyfingers. Spoon gelatin into pan. Sprinkle with chopped almonds. Chill until firm.

Makes 12 servings, each 157 calories; 13.5 grams protein; 6 grams fat; 12 grams carbohydrate. (With sugar, 301 calories)

> *1 serving = ½ bread exchange*
> *1 meat exchange*
> *½ cup skim milk*

Peach Cream Refrigerator Cake

This delectably smooth, rich-tasting dessert boasts of few calories but tastes like a million!

½ cup sour cream
4½ teaspoons liquid *Sucaryl*
½ teaspoon salt
½ teaspoon vanilla
¼ teaspoon almond extract
1 egg
1 envelope unflavored gelatin
¼ cup cold water
¼ cup nonfat dry milk
¼ cup ice water
2 cups sliced fresh peaches
2 tablespoons graham-cracker crumbs

Combine sour cream, *Sucaryl*, salt, vanilla, almond extract and egg; beat well. Soften gelatin in cold water; dissolve over boiling water. Add to sour-cream mixture; chill until slightly thickened. Combine dry milk and ice water; beat on high speed of mixer until of consistency of whipped cream; fold into gelatin mixture. Carefully fold in 1 cup sliced peaches. Spread cracker crumbs over bottom of a shallow 4-cup baking dish; spoon in gelatin mixture; chill until set. Garnish with remaining peach slices.

Makes 6 servings, each 106 calories; 5 grams protein; 5 grams fat; 10.5 grams carbohydrate. (With sugar, 214 calories)

1 serving = ½ fruit exchange
½ cup milk or ½ cup skim milk
+ 1 fat exchange

Hawaiian Refrigerator Cake

4 medium graham crackers, crushed
1 cup sour cream
3 tablespoons liquid *Sucaryl*
½ teaspoon salt
2 teaspoons vanilla
2 eggs
2 envelopes unflavored gelatin
½ cup cold water
2 8-ounce cans low-calorie
  pineapple tidbits, drained
½ cup nonfat dry milk
½ cup ice water

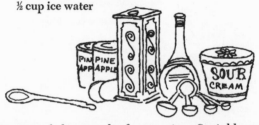

Reserve 2 tablespoons of the crumbs for topping. Sprinkle remainder evenly over the bottom of a lightly oiled 8-inch square baking pan. Combine sour cream, *Sucaryl*, salt, vanilla and eggs in small bowl of mixer. Blend until smooth. Soften gelatin in cold water and dissolve over hot water. Add to sour-cream mixture and chill until mixture begins to thicken. Chop pineapple into small pieces. Combine dry milk and ice water; beat on high speed of mixer until of consistency of whipped cream. Fold the whipped milk and chopped pineapple into gelatin mixture. Pour into crumb-lined pan. Sprinkle top with the reserved crumbs and chill until set.

Makes 9 servings, each 145 calories; 7 grams protein; 7 grams fat; 13.5 grams carbohydrate. (With sugar, 289 calories)

1 serving = 1 fat exchange
½ fruit exchange
½ cup milk or ½ cup skim milk
+ 1 fat exchange

Lemon Cheese Cake

2 envelopes unflavored gelatin
½ cup cold water
2 eggs, separated
¼ teaspoon salt
¾ cup lemon juice
3 tablespoons liquid *Sucaryl*
1 teaspoon grated lemon rind
1 teaspoon vanilla
3 cups skim-milk cottage
  cheese, sieved
⅓ cup nonfat dry milk
⅓ cup ice water
2 tablespoons crushed cornflakes

Soften gelatin in cold water. Combine egg yolks, salt, lemon juice and *Sucaryl* in top of double boiler. Cook over hot water, stirring constantly, until thick. Remove from heat; add softened gelatin, lemon rind and vanilla; stir to dissolve gelatin. Refrigerate until thick. Fold sieved cottage cheese into thickened gelatin. Beat egg whites until peaks form; fold into gelatin. Combine dry milk and ice water; beat on high speed of mixer until of consistency of whipped cream; fold into gelatin mixture. Lightly oil sides and bottom of a 9-inch round cake pan; sprinkle cornflake crumbs on sides only. Spoon cheese-cake mixture into pan; refrigerate until firm. Garnish, if desired, with dollops of Low-Calorie Whipped Topping, page 178, and tart jelly, or with *Sucaryl*-sweetened berries.

Makes 10 servings, each 106 calories; 17.5 grams protein; 1.5 grams fat; 5 grams carbohydrate. (With sugar, 236 calories)

1 serving = 1 meat exchange
½ cup skim milk

Chocolate Cheese Loaf

2 envelopes unflavored gelatin
¼ teaspoon salt
½ cup cocoa
3 tablespoons liquid *Sucaryl*
2 eggs, separated
1 cup skim milk
3 cups skim-milk cottage
   cheese, sieved
1 teaspoon vanilla
⅓ cup nonfat dry milk
⅓ cup ice water

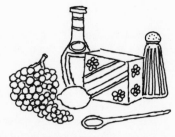

Place gelatin, salt and cocoa in top of double boiler. Combine *Sucaryl*, egg yolks and milk; blend into dry ingredients. Cook over boiling water, stirring constantly, until mixture thickens (about 10 minutes). Remove from heat; stir in sieved cottage cheese and vanilla; chill until mixture begins to mound. Beat egg whites until peaks form; fold into gelatin mixture. Combine dry milk and ice water; beat on high speed of mixer until of consistency of whipped cream. Fold into gelatin mixture. Turn into a lightly oiled loaf pan (11 × 4 × 2 inches). Chill until firm. Unmold and garnish, if desired, with Low-Calorie Whipped Topping, page 178, and shaved unsweetened chocolate.

Makes 12 servings, each 105 calories; 15.5 grams protein; 2.5 grams fat; 6 grams carbohydrate. (With sugar, 213 calories)

1 serving = 1 meat exchange
½ cup skim milk

Grapes in Wine Jelly

Get out an attractive mold for this shimmering wine dessert jelly. Note that calories have been reduced to considerably less than half the usual count.

> 2 envelopes unflavored gelatin
> ¼ cup cold water
> 1¾ cups boiling water
> 2 tablespoons liquid *Sucaryl*
> Dash of salt
> ¼ cup lemon juice
> 1¾ cups sauterne (14 ounces)
> 1 cup green seedless grapes

Soften gelatin in cold water; add boiling water, stirring until gelatin dissolves. Blend in *Sucaryl*, salt, lemon juice and sauterne. Chill until mixture begins to set; then fold in grapes. Pour into a lightly oiled 4-cup mold; chill until set. Unmold to serve. If desired, turn into glass serving bowl and break into tiny pieces with fork.

Makes 6 servings, each 86 calories; 3 grams protein; trace of fat; 7.5 grams carbohydrate. (With sugar, 230 calories)

Because of alcoholic content, consult physician before including in exchange system diet.

Rhubarb Strawberry Dessert Jelly

Forget the sugar, and save 288 calories in every tantalizingly sweet serving.

>   2 envelopes unflavored gelatin
>   ½ cup cold water
>   6 cups rhubarb, cut into 1-inch pieces
>   2 cups water
>   4 tablespoons liquid *Sucaryl*
>   Few drops of red food coloring
>   1 cup noncaloric lemon
>   carbonated beverage
>   2 cups strawberries, sliced

Soften gelatin in cold water. Combine rhubarb and the 2 cups water; cover and cook until tender; strain, saving only the liquid. Add to softened gelatin, stirring to dissolve. Add *Sucaryl*, and cool slightly. Stir in food coloring and carbonated beverage; chill until mixture begins to thicken. Fold in strawberries and pour into a lightly oiled 4-cup ring mold; chill until set. To serve, unmold and fill center with additional berries, if desired.

Makes 6 servings, each 48 calories; 4 grams protein; 0.5 gram fat; 9 grams carbohydrate. (With sugar, 336 calories)

1 serving = 1 fruit exchange

Orange Pineapple Jubilee

2 envelopes unflavored gelatin
¼ cup cold water
1 cup orange juice
½ cup sherry
¼ cup lemon juice
4 teaspoons liquid *Sucaryl*
1 cup orange sections
1 8½-ounce can low-calorie
   pineapple tidbits, drained

In a small bowl, soften gelatin in cold water. Bring orange juice to the boil, add to gelatin, stirring to dissolve. Add sherry, lemon juice and *Sucaryl;* chill until thick and syrupy. Add fruit; spoon into a lightly oiled 3-cup mold; chill until set.

Makes 5 servings, each 109 calories; 3 grams protein; trace of fat; 19 grams carbohydrate. (With sugar, 224 calories)

1 serving = 2 fruit exchanges

Frosted Lemon

Its sweet, vivacious flavor accented by fresh berries and fruits of your choice, this snowy pudding hardly knows the meaning of the word calorie!

2 envelopes unflavored gelatin
½ cup cold water
2 tablespoons liquid *Sucaryl*
1 cup boiling water
2 teaspoons grated lemon rind
⅓ cup lemon juice
3 egg whites

Soften gelatin in cold water; blend in *Sucaryl*, boiling water, lemon rind and juice; stir until gelatin dissolves. Refrigerate until mixture begins to set. Beat egg whites until stiff peaks form. Beat gelatin until foamy; fold in beaten egg whites. Spoon into a lightly oiled 4-cup mold; chill until set. To serve, unmold gelatin and garnish, if desired, with *Sucaryl*-sweetened berries or other fruit of the season.

Makes 6 servings, each 22 calories; 4.5 grams protein; no fat; 1 gram carbohydrate. (With sugar, 166 calories)

Need not be calculated as exchanges, if only one serving is used.

Jellied Plum Pudding

Unlike a steamed plum pudding (which, of course, never contains plums), this jellied dessert is made from tangy, full-flavored fresh plums.

> **3 envelopes unflavored gelatin**
> **1¼ cups cold water**
> **1½ pounds fresh plums, halved**
> ** and pitted**
> **1 cup unsweetened pineapple juice**
> **2 tablespoons liquid *Sucaryl***
> **2 egg whites**

Soften gelatin in ¾ cup of the cold water. In a saucepan, combine remaining ½ cup water and plums. Cover and cook until plums are tender. Purée plums; add hot purée to softened gelatin, stirring until gelatin dissolves. Blend in pineapple juice and *Sucaryl;* chill until mixture becomes thick and syrupy. Beat gelatin mixture until foamy; add egg whites, beating until mixture is thick and fluffy. Pour into a lightly oiled 5-cup mold; chill until set. If desired, serve with Low-Calorie Whipped Topping, page 178.

Makes 7 servings, each 78 calories; 5.5 grams protein; trace of fat; 15.5 grams carbohydrate. (With sugar, 201 calories)

1 serving = 2 fruit exchanges

Strawberries-in-the-Snow

This jewel-like dessert is molded in two layers—the top, pale pink and creamy; the bottom, sparkling red with sliced strawberries showing through.

3 envelopes unflavored gelatin	Few drops of red food coloring
½ cup cold water	2 3-ounce packages cream
4 cups boiling water	cheese
2 tablespoons liquid *Sucaryl*	2 cups sliced strawberries
2 tablespoons lemon juice	

Soften gelatin in cold water. Dissolve in boiling water. Add *Sucaryl*, lemon juice and food coloring. Add half the gelatin mixture very slowly to the softened cream cheese, blending until smooth. Pour into a lightly oiled 4-cup mold and chill until set. Add strawberries to remaining gelatin mixture. Pour over cream-cheese mixture and chill until set.

Makes 6 servings, each 142 calories; 7.5 grams protein; 10.5 grams fat; 5 grams carbohydrate. (With sugar, 286 calories)

> 1 serving = 1 fat exchange
> ½ fruit exchange
> 1 meat exchange

Double Apricot Mold

2 envelopes unflavored gelatin	2¾ teaspoons liquid *Sucaryl*
3 12-ounce cans low-calorie	¼ cup nonfat dry milk
apricot nectar	1 1-pound can low-calorie
2 tablespoons lemon juice	apricot halves, drained

Place gelatin in large bowl. Add 3 cups of the apricot nectar, lemon juice and 2 teaspoons *Sucaryl*. Heat 1 cup of the apricot nectar; add to gelatin mixture, stirring to dissolve. Pour into a lightly oiled 4-cup ring mold. Chill until set. Chill remaining ½ cup apricot nectar. At serving time, combine with the dry milk and the remaining ¾ teaspoon *Sucaryl*. Beat on high speed of mixer until of consistency of whipped cream. Unmold gelatin; fill center of ring with the apricot-flavored whipped topping. Arrange apricot halves around outside of mold.

Makes 6 servings, each 109 calories; 5.5 grams protein; trace of fat; 20 grams carbohydrate. (With sugar, 175 calories)

1 serving = 1½ fruit exchanges
½ cup skim milk

Fresh Plum Whip

Sweetness varies in different varieties of fresh plums. The blue-purple Italian prune-plum is generally sweet enough for eating out of hand. Others may be too sour to eat raw but are delicious cooked. Use fresh tart plums in this light-caloried whip.

> 2 envelopes unflavored gelatin
> 1 cup water
> 1½ pounds fresh tart plums,
>   pitted and halved
> 2 tablespoons liquid *Sucaryl*
> 1 tablespoon lemon juice
> 2 egg whites

Soften gelatin in ½ cup of the water. In saucepan, combine remaining ½ cup water and plums; cover and cook until plums are tender. Purée plums; add hot purée to softened gelatin, stirring until gelatin dissolves. Blend in *Sucaryl* and lemon juice; chill until mixture begins to set. Beat egg whites until stiff. Carefully fold chilled mixture into beaten egg whites. Chill until mixture begins to mound. Spoon into sherbet glasses; chill until set.

Makes 6 servings, each 66 calories; 4.5 grams protein; trace of fat; 12.5 grams carbohydrate. (With sugar, 210 calories)

1 serving = 1½ fruit exchanges

Cherry Pineapple Whip

Using the new blender method for gelatin desserts, this calorie-shy cherry treat requires no cooking, can be whipped together in minutes.

⅓ cup water
2 tablespoons liquid *Sucaryl*
1 tablespoon lemon juice
2 envelopes unflavored gelatin
¼ cup nonfat dry milk

½ cup hot, canned, unsweet-ened pineapple juice
1 1-pound can water-pack red sour cherries
2 cups crushed ice

Place all ingredients except cherries and ice in blender. Blend 1 minute. Add cherries and ice; blend 1 minute longer. Let mixture stand for a few minutes to set. Spoon into serving dishes.

Makes 6 servings, each 76 calories; 5.5 grams protein; 0.5 gram fat; 14.5 grams carbohydrate. (With sugar, 220 calories)

1 serving = 1 fruit exchange
½ cup skim milk

Cranberry Fluff

1 envelope unflavored gelatin
¼ cup cold water
2 cups cranberries
1½ cups orange juice
2 tablespoons liquid *Sucaryl*
¼ cup nonfat dry milk
¼ cup ice water

Soften gelatin in cold water. Combine cranberries, orange juice and *Sucaryl;* cook until skins pop. Drain, saving both liquid and berries. Add enough water to liquid to make 1½ cups; add soft-ened gelatin, stirring to dissolve. Chill until mixture begins to set; then beat until frothy. Combine dry milk and ice water; beat on high speed of mixer until of consistency of whipped cream; fold into gelatin mixture. Fold in cooked cranberries.

Chill until mixture just begins to set. Pile into sherbet or parfait glasses.

Makes 6 servings, each 68 calories; 4 grams protein; 0.5 gram fat; 13.5 grams carbohydrate. (With sugar, 212 calories)

½ serving = ½ fruit exchange
½ cup skim milk

Pink Pear Chiffon

4 pears, pared, halved and cored
1 cup water
1 tablespoon lemon juice
2 tablespoons liquid *Sucaryl*
2 cups strawberries
1 envelope unflavored gelatin
¼ cup cold water
½ cup nonfat dry milk
½ cup ice water

In saucepan, combine pears, 1 cup water, lemon juice and 1 tablespoon of the *Sucaryl*. Bring to the boil, reduce heat, cover and cook 10 to 15 minutes, or until pears are tender. Drain pears, reserving liquid. Crush strawberries; add enough of the pear liquid to measure 3 cups. Soften gelatin in ¼ cup cold water; dissolve over boiling water. Add to strawberry mixture with remaining tablespoon of *Sucaryl;* chill until mixture thickens slightly. Combine dry milk and ice water; beat on high speed of mixer until peaks form; fold into gelatin. Coarsely chop pears; fold into gelatin. Spoon into dessert bowl or individual sherbet glasses. Chill.

Makes 8 servings, each 93 calories; 4.5 grams protein; 0.5 gram fat; 19 grams carbohydrate. (With sugar, 201 calories)

1 serving = 1½ fruit exchanges
½ cup skim milk

Chilled Lemon Soufflé

Chilled dessert soufflés are dreamy affairs, and have the cool advantage of being prepared early in the day, to be produced with a flourish at dinnertime. One hostess we know rates this Chilled Lemon Soufflé as her favorite party dessert.

2 envelopes unflavored gelatin
½ cup cold water
8 eggs, separated
4 tablespoons liquid *Sucaryl*
½ teaspoon salt
2 teaspoons grated lemon rind
1 cup lemon juice
½ cup nonfat dry milk
½ cup ice water

Fasten a 6-inch band of foil around a 6-cup soufflé dish, allowing 4 inches to stand above top of dish. Soften gelatin in cold water. Combine egg yolks, *Sucaryl*, salt, lemon rind and lemon juice in top of a double boiler. Cook over hot water, stirring occasionally, until thick. Remove from heat; add softened gelatin, stirring to dissolve. Chill until mixture begins to thicken. Beat egg whites stiff; fold into gelatin mixture. Combine dry milk and ice water; beat on high speed of mixer until stiff, about 10 minutes; fold into gelatin. Gently spoon into soufflé dish; chill several hours until set. Remove foil before serving.

Makes 10 servings, each 96 calories; 9 grams protein; 4.5 grams fat; 5 grams carbohydrate. (With sugar, 268 calories)

1 serving = 1 meat exchange
¼ cup skim milk

Cold Sherry Soufflé

2 envelopes unflavored gelatin
½ cup cold water
1½ cups sherry
5 eggs, separated
1 tablespoon lemon juice
1½ tablespoons liquid *Sucaryl*
10 ladyfingers, split

Fasten a 4-inch band of foil around a 6-cup soufflé dish, allowing 2 inches to stand above top of dish. Soften gelatin in cold water; dissolve over boiling water. Add sherry and chill until mixture begins to thicken. Beat egg whites until foamy; add lemon juice and beat until stiff. Beat egg yolks until frothy; add *Sucaryl* and beat on high speed of mixer until thick and lemon-colored (about 5 minutes). Fold beaten egg whites into beaten yolks. Fold egg mixture into gelatin mixture. Place ladyfingers around edge of soufflé dish. Carefully pour in soufflé mixture. Chill until firm. Remove foil before serving. If desired, garnish with Low-Calorie Whipped Topping, page 178.

Makes 10 servings, each 115 calories; 5.5 grams protein; 3 grams fat; 7 grams carbohydrate. (With sugar, 180 calories)

1 serving = ½ bread exchange
½ meat exchange

Because of alcoholic content, consult with physician before including in exchange-system diet.

Eggnog Soufflé Glacé

2 envelopes unflavored gelatin
½ cup cold water
6 eggs, separated
2 cups skim milk
2 tablespoons liquid *Sucaryl*
1 teaspoon vanilla
¼ cup rum
½ cup nonfat dry milk
½ cup ice water

Fasten a 6-inch band of foil around a 4-cup soufflé dish, allowing 4 inches to stand above top of dish. Soften gelatin in cold water. Combine egg yolks, milk, *Sucaryl* and vanilla in top of double boiler; blend well. Cook over hot water, stirring occasionally, until slightly thickened. Remove from heat; add softened gelatin and rum, stirring until gelatin dissolves. Chill until mixture begins to mound from spoon. Beat egg whites until soft peaks form; fold into gelatin mixture. Combine dry milk and ice water; beat on high speed of mixer until of consistency of whipped cream; fold into gelatin. Gently spoon into soufflé dish; chill several hours until firm. Remove foil before serving. If desired, garnish with Low-Calorie Whipped Topping, page 178, and shaved chocolate.

Makes 8 servings, each 132 calories; 11.5 grams protein; 4 grams fat; 7 grams carbohydrate. (With sugar, 240 calories)

1 serving = 1 meat exchange
½ cup skim milk

Chocolate Marble Soufflé

3 envelopes unflavored gelatin
½ cup cold water
8 eggs, separated
7½ teaspoons liquid *Sucaryl*
2 cups skim milk
1 teaspoon vanilla
½ cup cocoa
½ cup nonfat dry milk
½ cup ice water

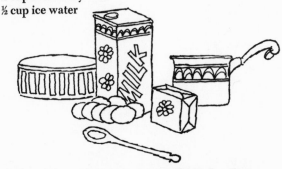

Fasten a 6-inch band of foil around a 6-cup soufflé dish, allowing 4 inches to stand above top of dish. Soften gelatin in cold water. Combine egg yolks, *Sucaryl,* milk and vanilla in top of a double boiler; blend well. Cook over hot water, stirring occasionally, until thick. Remove from heat; add softened gelatin, stirring to dissolve. Chill until mixture begins to thicken. Divide mixture into two bowls. Blend cocoa into mixture in one bowl. Beat egg whites stiff; fold half into each mixture. Combine dry milk and ice water; beat on high speed of mixer until stiff, about 10 minutes. Gently fold half into each mixture. Alternately spoon vanilla and chocolate mixtures into prepared soufflé dish to create a marbled effect. Chill several hours until set. Remove foil before serving.

Makes 10 servings, each 127 calories; 11.5 grams protein; 6 grams fat; 8.5 grams carbohydrate. (With sugar, 235 calories)

1 serving = 1 meat exchange
½ cup skim milk

DESSERTS, FROZEN

Banana Ice Milk
Strawberry Ice Milk
Chocolate Ice Milk
Orange Sherbet
Pineapple Sherbet

Pineapple-Grapefruit Sherbet
Pineapple-Orange Sherbet
Orange-Grapefruit Sherbet
Frozen Chocolate Mousse

Many will remember with nostalgia the excitement and anticipation of awaiting a dish of homemade ice cream from the hand-cranked ice cream freezer. When the crank refused to budge one more inch, out would come the dasher covered with the creamiest, most delicious ice cream you ever tasted.

Hardware and department stores today stock a fascinating array of old-fashioned hand-turned ice cream freezers, as well as motor-driven electric models. And the pleasures of homemade frozen desserts are just as great as they used to be. Most manufacturers include a booklet of recipes, but for those interested in curbing calories, the low-calorie recipes given here will be of especial interest. Made with calorie-free sweetening rather than with sugar, and with skim milk instead of heavy cream, these "ice milks" are so deliciously creamy, smooth and rich-tasting, you'll find it hard to believe the calorie-laden ingredients have been eliminated.

All of the low-calorie "ice milk" recipes yield 2 to 2½ pints, and may be made in either a 2-quart or 4-quart ice cream freezer. If you prefer to make a larger quantity, simply increase the ingredients proportionately. In the event any is not finished off in the first serving, pack the remainder in freezer boxes for storage in your freezer. Unlike most sugarless frozen desserts, these remain smooth and creamy after freezer storage. They will be somewhat harder when first removed from the freezer, so allow a few minutes for softening before serving.

Also included are directions for some remarkably creamy and rich-tasting fruit sherbets which may be frozen in the freezer compartment of your refrigerator or in your home freezer. These sugar-free sherbets have been calorie-slashed to approximately half their usual calorie counts.

Banana Ice Milk

> 1 envelope unflavored gelatin
> ½ cup cold water
> 2 cups skim milk, scalded
> ¾ cup nonfat dry milk
> 4½ teaspoons liquid *Sucaryl*
> 1 tablespoon lemon juice
> 2 teaspoons vanilla
> 2 medium bananas, mashed

Soften gelatin in cold water. Combine scalded milk, dry milk, *Sucaryl*, lemon juice and vanilla. Add softened gelatin, stirring to dissolve. Chill until mixture begins to thicken. Fold in mashed bananas. Pour into electric ice cream freezer. Freeze, using 8 parts ice to 1 part rock salt. Freezer will stop when ice milk is done (about 20 minutes).

Makes 2½ pints or 5 servings, each 143 calories; 12 grams protein; 0.5 gram fat; 24 grams carbohydrate. (With sugar, 272 calories)

> *1 serving = ½ fruit exchange*
> *1½ cups skim milk*

STRAWBERRY ICE MILK: Follow directions for Banana Ice Milk, increasing *Sucaryl* to 2 tablespoons and replacing bananas with 2 cups strawberries, crushed. Freezing time will be about 30 minutes.

Makes 2½ pints or 5 servings, each 129 calories; 12 grams protein; 0.5 gram fat; 19.5 grams carbohydrate. (With sugar, 302 calories)

1 serving = 1½ cups skim milk

CHOCOLATE ICE MILK: Follow directions for Banana Ice Milk, increasing *Sucaryl* to 2 tablespoons, omitting lemon juice, decreasing vanilla to 1 teaspoon and replacing banana with 1 ounce unsweetened chocolate, melted. Beat with rotary beater to blend in chocolate. Freezing time will be about 30 minutes.

Makes 2 pints or 4 servings, each 169 calories; 15 grams protein; 4 grams fat; 20 grams carbohydrate. (With sugar, 385 calories)

1 serving = 1 fat exchange
1½ cups skim milk

Orange Sherbet

> 1 14½-ounce can evaporated
> milk, well chilled
> 2 tablespoons liquid *Sucaryl*
> 1 6-ounce can unsweetened
> frozen orange juice concen-
> trate, thawed

Beat chilled evaporated milk until stiff. Gradually add *Sucaryl* and thawed orange juice concentrate, blending well. Spoon into 3 1-pint plastic freezer cartons, and freeze.

Makes 6 servings, each 148 calories; 5 grams protein; 5 grams fat; 20 grams carbohydrate. (With sugar, 294 calories)

> *1 serving = 1½ fruit exchanges*
> *½ cup milk*

PINEAPPLE SHERBET: Follow directions for Orange Sherbet, replacing orange juice concentrate with 1 6-ounce can unsweetened frozen pineapple juice concentrate.

Makes 6 servings, each 168 calories; 5 grams protein; 6 grams fat; 24 grams carbohydrate. (With sugar, 312 calories)

> *1 serving = 2 fruit exchanges*
> *½ cup milk*

PINEAPPLE-GRAPEFRUIT SHERBET: Follow directions for Orange Sherbet, replacing orange juice concentrate with 1 6-ounce can unsweetened frozen pineapple-grapefruit juice concentrate.

Makes 6 servings, each 144 calories; 5 grams protein; 6 grams fat; 20 grams carbohydrate. (With sugar, 288 calories)

> *1 serving = 1½ fruit exchanges*
> *½ cup milk*

PINEAPPLE-ORANGE SHERBET: Follow directions for Orange Sherbet, replacing orange juice concentrate with 1 6-ounce can unsweetened frozen pineapple-orange juice concentrate.

Makes 6 servings, each 144 calories; 5 grams protein; 5.5 grams fat; 20 grams carbohydrate. (With sugar, 288 calories)

1 serving = 1½ fruit exchanges
½ cup milk

ORANGE-GRAPEFRUIT SHERBET: Follow directions for Orange Sherbet, replacing orange juice concentrate with 1 6-ounce can unsweetened orange-grapefruit juice concentrate.

Makes 6 servings, each 158 calories; 6 grams protein; 6 grams fat; 23 grams carbohydrate. (With sugar, 302 calories)

1 serving = 1½ fruit exchanges
½ cup milk

Frozen Chocolate Mousse

1 teaspoon unflavored gelatin
2 tablespoons water
1 ounce unsweetened chocolate
¼ cup hot water
¼ teaspoon salt
1 tablespoon liquid *Sucaryl*
1 teaspoon vanilla
⅔ cup ice water
⅛ teaspoon cream of tartar
⅔ cup nonfat dry milk

Soften gelatin in 2 tablespoons water; set aside. Melt chocolate in top of double boiler over gently boiling water; add hot water; stir until smooth; remove from heat. Add softened gelatin; stir until dissolved. Add salt, *Sucaryl* and vanilla; chill until mixture begins to thicken slightly. Combine ice water and cream of tartar in small mixer bowl; add dry milk, and beat 5 minutes on high speed of mixer until stiff peaks form. Gently fold in chocolate mixture. Pour into a 1-quart mold. Freeze 6 hours, or until firm.

Makes 4 servings, each 110 calories; 8 grams protein; 4 grams fat; 12.5 grams carbohydrate. (With sugar, 218 calories)

1 serving = 1 fat exchange
1 cup skim milk

DESSERTS, FRUITS

Dieter's Applesauce
Cranberry Applesauce
Spiced Rhubarb Sauce
Old-Fashioned Fruit Pudding
Gingered Pear Compote
Rhubarb Strawberry Compote
Peaches and Raspberries in Port
Chilled Peaches Cardinale
Summer Fruits Sauterne
Four-Fruit Medley with Rum

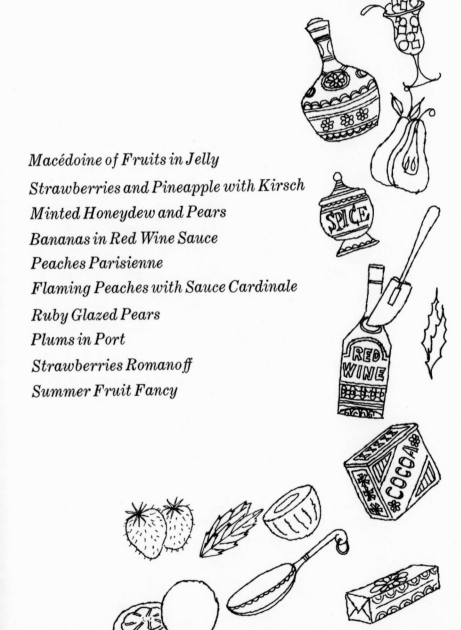

Macédoine of Fruits in Jelly

Strawberries and Pineapple with Kirsch

Minted Honeydew and Pears

Bananas in Red Wine Sauce

Peaches Parisienne

Flaming Peaches with Sauce Cardinale

Ruby Glazed Pears

Plums in Port

Strawberries Romanoff

Summer Fruit Fancy

Dieter's Applesauce

2 pounds cooking apples, quartered
½ cup water
1 tablespoon liquid *Sucaryl*
1 tablespoon lemon juice

Combine apples and water in saucepan; cover and simmer 15 to 20 minutes, or until tender. Force through food mill. Stir in *Sucaryl* and lemon juice.

Makes 6 servings, each 78 calories; 0.5 gram protein; 0.5 gram fat; 20 grams carbohydrate. (With sugar, 150 calories)

1 serving = 2 fruit exchanges

Cranberry Applesauce

1 pound (4 cups) raw cranberries
2 pounds cooking apples, pared and diced
1¼ cups water
⅛ teaspoon salt
5 tablespoons liquid *Sucaryl*

Combine all ingredients in a large saucepan. Cover and cook slowly 15 to 20 minutes, or until apples are tender and berries pop. Crush fruits and chill.

Makes 8 half-cup servings, each 85 calories; 0.5 gram protein; 1 gram fat; 21 grams carbohydrate. (With sugar, 355 calories)

1 serving = 2 fruit exchanges

Spiced Rhubarb Sauce

1½ pounds rhubarb
½ cup water
½ cup vinegar
½ teaspoon ginger

½ teaspoon cinnamon
¼ teaspoon cloves
4 tablespoons liquid *Sucaryl*

Cut rhubarb into 1-inch pieces. Do not peel pink, tender rhubarb. Place in a large saucepan with remaining ingredients. Cover and simmer for 20 to 25 minutes, or until rhubarb is tender. Chill before serving.

Makes 8 half-cup servings, each 11 calories; trace protein; no fat; 3 grams carbohydrate. (With sugar, 227 calories)

Need not be calculated as exchanges.

Old-Fashioned Fruit Pudding

1 1-pound can low-calorie
  apricot halves
2 8-ounce cans low-calorie
  Kadota figs
1 1-pound can low-calorie
  Royal Anne cherries

1 8-ounce can low-calorie
  Bartlett pears
1½ tablespoons liquid *Sucaryl*
4 tablespoons quick-cooking
  tapioca

Drain fruits, saving liquid. Place fruits in a dessert bowl. Measure 2 cups of the combined liquids; pour into a saucepan. Add *Sucaryl* and tapioca; let stand 5 minutes. Cook, stirring constantly, until thick and clear. Pour sauce over fruit. Chill. If desired, serve with Custard Sauce, page 175.

Makes 8 servings, each 104 calories; 1 gram protein; trace of fat; 23.5 grams carbohydrate. (With sugar, 185 calories)

*1 serving = ½ bread exchange
1½ fruit exchanges*

Gingered Pear Compote

1 cup water	Rind of 1 lemon, cut into strips
7 ounces (14 tablespoons) sauterne	6 ripe pears, pared, quartered and cored
4 tablespoons liquid *Sucaryl*	1½ tablespoons cornstarch
1 teaspoon ground ginger	Grated rind of 1 orange

In a saucepan, combine water, sauterne, *Sucaryl*, ginger and lemon rind; bring to the boil. Add quartered pears, a few at a time; cover and simmer until tender (about 8 to 10 minutes). With a slotted spoon, remove pears to a serving dish; discard lemon peel. Mix a small amount of cold water into the cornstarch to make a smooth paste; gradually blend into the hot liquid. Cook, stirring constantly, over medium heat until thickened, 8 to 10 minutes. Pour sauce over fruit. Serve warm or cold, sprinkling with grated orange rind just before serving.

Makes 8 servings, each 98 calories; 1 gram protein; 0.5 gram fat; 20 grams carbohydrate. (With sugar, 314 calories)

1 serving = 2 fruit exchanges

Rhubarb Strawberry Compote

1 pound fresh rhubarb, cut into ½-inch pieces
3 tablespoons liquid *Sucaryl*
1 tablespoon grated orange rind
½ cup orange juice
1 pint fresh strawberries, hulled
1 tablespoon lemon juice

In saucepan, combine rhubarb, 2 tablespoons of the *Sucaryl*, orange rind and juice. Cover and simmer about 10 minutes, or until rhubarb is tender but not mushy. Remove from heat and cool. Sprinkle strawberries with remaining 1 tablespoon *Sucaryl* and lemon juice. Combine with rhubarb in serving dish. Chill well before serving.

Makes 8 servings, each 27 calories; 0.5 gram protein; trace of fat; 6.5 grams carbohydrate. (With sugar, 189 calories)

1 serving = ½ fruit exchange

Peaches and Raspberries in Port

If you're partial to peaches and mad for raspberries, mix them amicably, as directed here. When surreptitiously sweetened with *Sucaryl,* each serving is calorie-trimmed of more than 100 calories.

> 4½ teaspoons liquid *Sucaryl*
> 1 cup water
> 2 slices fresh lemon
> 3 cups peeled, sliced fresh peaches
> 2 teaspoons cornstarch
> 1 cup fresh red raspberries
> 1 wineglass (3½ ounces) port wine

Combine *Sucaryl,* water and lemon slices in saucepan. Bring to the boil. Add peaches and simmer, covered, over low heat 5 minutes, or until peaches are tender. Remove from heat. With a slotted spoon, remove peaches from liquid and place in serving dish. Mix cornstarch with a little cold water to make a paste. Add to hot liquid and cook until sauce is thickened. Remove from heat, and while the sauce is still warm, but off the heat, add the raspberries. Add wine. Pour the raspberry sauce over the peaches. Remove lemon slices. Chill before serving.

Makes 6 servings, each 80 calories; 0.5 gram protein; trace of fat; 16 grams carbohydrate. (With sugar, 188 calories)

1 serving = 1½ fruit exchanges

Chilled Peaches Cardinale

1 pint fresh raspberries
1¼ cups water
2½ tablespoons liquid *Sucaryl*
1 tablespoon lemon juice
2 pints strawberries
8 ripe peaches, peeled and halved

Buzz raspberries and ¼ cup water in blender, or put through sieve or food mill. (Strain to remove seeds if blender is used.) Add ½ tablespoon of the *Sucaryl* and lemon juice. Wash, hull and slice strawberries; sprinkle with ½ tablespoon *Sucaryl*. Mix raspberry sauce with sweetened strawberries; chill. Combine remaining 1 cup water and the remaining 1½ tablespoons *Sucaryl* in a large saucepan; bring to the boil. Add peaches and simmer, covered, over low heat 5 minutes, or until tender. Remove peaches with a slotted spoon; place in dessert bowl or individual dishes and chill well. Before serving, top with berry sauce.

Makes 8 servings, each 91 calories; 1.5 grams protein; 0.5 gram fat; 22.5 grams carbohydrate. (With sugar, 226 calories)

1 serving = 2½ fruit exchanges

Summer Fruits Sauterne

> 1 cup blueberries
> 1 cup strawberries
> 1 cup sweet cherries, pitted
> 1 tablespoon liquid *Sucaryl*
> 3½ ounces (7 tablespoons) sauterne
> 2 medium bananas, sliced

Combine all ingredients except bananas; chill in refrigerator several hours. Just before serving, add sliced bananas. If desired, garnish top lightly with shredded coconut.*

Makes 6 servings, each 82 calories; 1 gram protein; 0.5 gram fat; 17.5 grams carbohydrate. (With sugar, 154 calories)

1 serving = 2 fruit exchanges

* *For each tablespoon dried shredded coconut, add 21 calories.*

Four-Fruit Medley with Rum

2 medium oranges	3 tablespoons lemon juice
½ cantaloupe	1½ teaspoons liquid *Sucaryl*
2 ripe pears	¼ teaspoon mace
½ pound seedless grapes	1 ounce (2 tablespoons) rum
2 tablespoons grated orange rind	

Peel and section oranges. Cut cantaloupe into balls and pears into cubes. Combine all fruits in large bowl. Add orange rind, lemon juice, *Sucaryl*, mace and rum; mix lightly. Chill before serving.

Makes 4 cups or 8 servings, each 74 calories; 1 gram protein; trace of fat; 16.5 grams carbohydrate. (With sugar, 101 calories)

1 serving = 1½ fruit exchanges

Macédoine of Fruits in Jelly

1 8½-ounce can low-calorie
pineapple tidbits
1 8-ounce can low-calorie
sliced peaches
1½ tablespoons unflavored
gelatin
1¼ cups unsweetened
grapefruit juice
2 tablespoons liquid *Sucaryl*
½ cup rosé wine
Few drops of red food coloring
2 medium bananas, sliced
diagonally
2 pears, pared, cored and diced
1 cup seedless grapes
1 cup orange sections

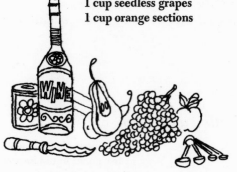

Drain pineapple and peaches; set fruit aside. Soften gelatin in liquid from fruit. Bring grapefruit juice to the boil; add to softened gelatin, stirring to dissolve gelatin. Add *Sucaryl*, wine and food coloring, as desired. Refrigerate 45 minutes. Meanwhile, place fruit in an 8-cup compote or brandy snifter; pour chilled gelatin over fruit. Refrigerate until gelatin thickens. (Gelatin will become thick, but not firmly set.)

Makes 6 servings, each 171 calories; 4 grams protein; 0.5 gram fat; 36.5 grams carbohydrate. (With sugar, 315 calories)

1 serving = 4 fruit exchanges

Strawberries and Pineapple with Kirsch

> 2 8-ounce cans low-calorie
>   pineapple tidbits
> 4 cups hulled strawberries
> 2 tablespoons liquid *Sucaryl*
> 3 tablespoons kirsch

Combine all ingredients; chill several hours. Garnish with mint, if desired.

Makes 6 servings, each 91 calories; 1 gram protein; 1 gram fat; 16.5 grams carbohydrate. (With sugar, 235 calories)

1 serving = 2 fruit exchanges

Minted Honeydew and Pears

This artistic presentation of two of our most succulent fruits will delight the dieter. Each serving adds up to less than half the usual calorie tab.

> 1½ cups fresh ripe pear slices
> 2 cups honeydew melon balls
> ⅓ cup lemon juice
> 1 tablespoon liquid *Sucaryl*
> 1 tablespoon chopped mint leaves

Combine all ingredients and mix well. Chill for 3 to 4 hours before serving. Garnish with sprigs of fresh mint.

Makes 6 servings, each 62 calories; 1 gram protein; trace of fat; 15 grams carbohydrate. (With sugar, 134 calories)

1 serving = 1½ fruit exchanges

Bananas in Red Wine Sauce

This is a simple but elegant party dessert to delight dieters and nondieters alike. And look at the calorie savings!

>   4 medium bananas
>   2 tablespoons butter
>   1 cup claret wine
>   1 tablespoon cornstarch
>   2 tablespoons liquid *Sucaryl*
>   Dash of nutmeg

Lightly brown peeled whole bananas in butter. In a saucepan, add a little of the wine to the cornstarch to make a smooth paste; stir in remaining wine. Add *Sucaryl;* cook over medium heat, stirring constantly, until thick and clear. Add nutmeg. Pour over bananas and simmer for several minutes. Serve warm.

Makes 4 servings, each 188 calories; 1 gram protein; 6 grams fat; 25 grams carbohydrate. (With sugar, 404 calories)

>   *1 serving = 1 fat exchange*
>   *2½ fruit exchanges*

Because of alcoholic content, consult physician before including in exchange-system diet.

Peaches Parisienne

>   2 tablespoons liquid *Sucaryl*
>   ¼ cup water
>   6 red, sour plums
>   8 ripe peaches
>   ½ cup peach brandy

Combine *Sucaryl*, water and plums in saucepan. Cook, covered, over medium heat until skins burst and juice is red. Put through sieve or food mill; chill. Peel peaches and cut in half. Brush with a little lemon juice to prevent darkening. Pour brandy over peach halves. Let chill several hours. When ready to serve, place peach halves in sherbet glasses or in a compote dish. Pour plum sauce over peaches.

Makes 8 servings, each 103 calories; 1 gram protein; trace of fat; 17.5 grams carbohydrate. (With sugar, 211 calories)

1 serving = 2 fruit exchanges

Flaming Peaches with Sauce Cardinale

1 cup strawberries
1 cup red raspberries
3 tablespoons liquid *Sucaryl*
1 teaspoon cornstarch
2 ounces (4 tablespoons) brandy
6 ripe peaches, peeled and halved

Combine strawberries and ½ cup of the raspberries in blender; run a few seconds until puréed. Measure and add enough water to make 2 cups. Make a paste of the *Sucaryl* and cornstarch in top pan, or blazer, of a chafing dish. Add puréed fruits. Place pan over direct flame. Bring to the boil and cook until thickened. Stir in 1 ounce (2 tablespoons) of the brandy. Add the peach halves, basting peaches with the sauce. (This part of the process may be completed in advance, if desired.) At serving time, heat peaches and sauce; add remaining ½ cup whole raspberries. Warm the remaining 1 ounce brandy in a large spoon or ladle over a candle or flame. Ignite. Pour over fruit and stir to blend.

Makes 6 servings, each 93 calories; 1 gram protein; 0.5 gram fat; 17 grams carbohydrate. (With sugar, 309 calories)

1 serving = 2 fruit exchanges

Ruby Glazed Pears

4 pears, pared, halved and cored
2 tablespoons lemon juice
1 cup boiling water

2 tablespoons liquid *Sucaryl*
2 cups unsweetened frozen
  strawberries, thawed
2 tablespoons sherry

Preheat oven to 350°F. Place pears in shallow baking dish; sprinkle with lemon juice to prevent browning. Combine boiling water and 1 tablespoon of the *Sucaryl*. Pour over pears; cover and bake 30 to 45 minutes, or until pears are tender. Cool in this liquid. Purée strawberries; add sherry and remaining 1 tablespoon *Sucaryl*. Place pears in strawberry mixture; chill, turning occasionally to coat evenly. Serve with sauce.

Makes 4 servings, each 134 calories; 1.5 grams protein; 1 gram fat; 31.5 grams carbohydrate. (With sugar, 350 calories)

1 serving = 3 fruit exchanges

Plums in Port

12 whole fresh plums
3 cups water

4 tablespoons liquid *Sucaryl*
¾ cup (6 ounces) port wine

Wash plums. Combine remaining ingredients in a large saucepan; bring to the boil. Reduce heat; add plums and simmer gently, about 5 minutes, or until tender. Remove from heat. Chill before serving.

Makes 6 servings, each 104 calories; 1 gram protein; trace of fat; 19 grams carbohydrate. (With sugar, 393 calories)

1 serving = 2 fruit exchanges

Strawberries Romanoff

2 cups sliced strawberries
1 tablespoon liquid *Sucaryl*
2 ounces (4 tablespoons) orange curaçao

¼ cup nonfat dry milk
¼ cup ice water

Combine strawberries, *Sucaryl* and orange curaçao. Chill for several hours. Before serving, combine dry milk and icê water; beat on high speed of mixer until of consistency of whipped cream. Fold into strawberries. Spoon into sherbet glasses and serve at once.

Makes 4 servings, each 97 calories; 3 grams protein; 0.5 gram fat; 13 grams carbohydrate. (With sugar, 205 calories)

1 serving = 1 fruit exchange
¼ cup skim milk

Summer Fruit Fancy

A mixture of ice-cold fruits, flavored with orange liqueur and covered with a snowy cloud of whipped topping and melted chocolate.

1 pint red raspberries	½ recipe Low-Calorie Whipped
3 cups peeled and sliced ripe peaches	Topping, page 178
	1 ounce unsweetened chocolate, grated
½ pound seedless green grapes	
4½ teaspoons liquid *Sucaryl*	
2 ounces (4 tablespoons) orange curaçao	

Sprinkle raspberries over peaches. Add grapes, *Sucaryl* and orange curaçao. Chill until mixture is very cold. Just before serving, heat broiler. Spoon fruit into heatproof dessert dishes. Top· with whipped topping and sprinkle with grated chocolate. Place under broiler *just* until chocolate melts (about 30 seconds). Serve immediately.

Makes 8 servings, each 118 calories; 2.5 grams protein; 2 grams fat; 21 grams carbohydrate. (With sugar, 212 calories)

1 serving = ½ fat exchange
2 fruit exchanges

DESSERT SAUCES

Stirred Custard Sauce
Chocolate Sauce
Lemon Pudding Sauce
Creamy Maple Dessert Sauce
Foamy Brandy Sauce
Orange Dessert Sauce
Cherry-Almond Dessert Sauce
Strawberry-Sherry Sauce
Low-Calorie Whipped Topping

TOPPINGS, FILLINGS

Cheese Dessert Topping
Rum-Flavored Whipped Topping
Brandy-Flavored Whipped Topping
Orange-Flavored Whipped Topping
Thick Custard Cream (Crème Pâtissière)
Lemon Custard Cream
Custard Chiffon
Lemon Custard Chiffon

Chocolate Sauce

1 tablespoon butter	1 cup skim milk
2 tablespoons cocoa	2 teaspoons liquid *Sucaryl*
1 tablespoon cornstarch	½ teaspoon vanilla
Dash of salt	

Melt butter in a small saucepan over low heat. Combine cocoa, cornstarch and salt; blend with melted butter until smooth. Add milk and *Sucaryl;* cook over moderate heat, stirring constantly, until slightly thickened; remove from heat. Stir in vanilla. Cool. (Sauce thickens as it cools.)

Makes 1 cup, each ¼-cup serving 64 calories; 2.5 grams protein; 3.5 grams fat; 6.5 grams carbohydrate. (With sugar, 136 calories)

1 serving = ½ cup milk or ½ cup skim milk
+ 1 fat exchange

Lemon Pudding Sauce

1 tablespoon cornstarch	1 tablespoon liquid *Sucaryl*
¼ cup lemon juice	1 tablespoon butter
Rind of 1 lemon	Dash of salt
¾ cup water	Dash of nutmeg

Place cornstarch in small saucepan; blend in lemon juice to make a smooth paste. Add lemon rind, water and *Sucaryl.* Cook over medium heat, stirring constantly until thickened. Remove from heat and blend in butter, salt and nutmeg. Serve warm over fruit, cottage pudding, gingerbread, fruit cobbler, cake.

Makes 1 cup, each ¼-cup serving 36 calories; no protein; 3 grams fat; 3 grams carbohydrate. (With sugar, 144 calories)

1 serving = 1 fat exchange

If used in larger amounts, ½ cup = ½ bread exchange
1 fat exchange

Creamy Maple Dessert Sauce

¼ cup butter
2 tablespoons flour
2 tablespoons liquid *Sucaryl*

½ cup water
1 cup evaporated milk
1½ teaspoons maple flavoring

Melt butter; blend in flour; add *Sucaryl,* water and evaporated milk. Cook over medium heat, stirring constantly until thickened. Remove from heat and add flavoring. Chill.

Makes 1½ cups, each ¼-cup serving 133 calories; 3 grams protein; 11 grams fat; 6 grams carbohydrate. (With sugar, 277 calories)

1 serving = 1 fat exchange
½ cup milk

Stirred Custard Sauce (*English Custard*)

3 cups skim milk
1 tablespoon liquid *Sucaryl*
2 tablespoons flour

5 egg yolks
1 teaspoon vanilla

In top of double boiler, combine milk and *Sucaryl;* heat. Combine flour and egg yolks; beat well. Add a small amount of the hot milk to the egg mixture, blending well. Return mixture to top of double boiler. Cook over simmering water, stirring constantly, until mixture thickens slightly (about 15 minutes). Immediately remove from heat; pour into heatproof bowl and stir in flavoring. Place in refrigerator to chill rapidly. (Custard thickens more as it chills.)

Makes 3½ cups, each half-cup serving 88 calories; 6 grams protein; 4 grams fat; 7 grams carbohydrate. (With sugar, 150 calories)

1 serving = ½ cup milk or ½ cup skim milk
+ 1 fat exchange

Foamy Brandy Sauce

¾ cup skim milk, scalded
2 egg yolks, well beaten
1½ teaspoons liquid *Sucaryl*
¼ teaspoon vanilla
2 tablespoons cognac
2 egg whites, stiffly beaten

Gradually blend scalded milk into the well-beaten egg yolks in a saucepan. Add *Sucaryl;* cook over medium heat, stirring constantly, only until mixture coats a silver spoon. Remove from heat; blend in vanilla, cognac and stiffly beaten egg whites. Serve warm.

Makes 2½ cups, each ¼-cup serving 28 calories; 2 grams protein; 1 gram fat; 1 gram carbohydrate. (With sugar, 50 calories)

½ cup = ½ meat exchange

Orange Dessert Sauce

1½ cups orange juice
½ teaspoon grated orange rind
2 tablespoons cornstarch
1 tablespoon liquid *Sucaryl*
Dash of salt
1 large orange, sectioned

Combine all ingredients (except orange sections) in small saucepan. Cook over medium heat, stirring constantly, until thick. Add orange sections; cool.

Makes 1¾ cups sauce, each ¼-cup serving 46 calories; 0.5 gram protein; trace of fat; 11.5 grams carbohydrate. (With sugar, 108 calories)

1 serving = 1 fruit exchange

Cherry-Almond Dessert Sauce

2 cups canned water-pack red
  sour cherries
4 teaspoons cornstarch
1 tablespoon liquid *Sucaryl*
¼ teaspoon almond extract
1 tablespoon lemon juice

Drain cherries and set aside. Measure cherry liquid and add water to make 1½ cups. Gradually blend into cornstarch in saucepan. Add *Sucaryl;* cook until clear and thick; then add lemon juice and almond extract. Add cherries and heat through. Serve warm.

Makes 3 cups, each ¼-cup serving 24 calories; 0.5 gram protein; trace of fat; 6 grams carbohydrate. (With sugar, 60 calories)

1 serving = ½ fruit exchange

Strawberry-Sherry Sauce

5 cups hulled strawberries,
  whole or sliced
1 tablespoon cornstarch
7½ teaspoons liquid *Sucaryl*
3 tablespoons sherry

Crush 1 cup of the strawberries; force through sieve; measure and add enough water to make 1 cup. Slowly stir into cornstarch in small saucepan; cook over medium heat, stirring constantly, until thick. Remove from heat; add *Sucaryl* and sherry; cool slightly. Pour sauce over remaining berries; chill.

Makes 4 cups, each half-cup serving 45 calories; 1 gram protein; 0.5 gram fat; 9 grams carbohydrate. (With sugar, 179 calories)

1 serving = 1 fruit exchange

Low-Calorie Whipped Topping

½ cup nonfat dry milk
½ cup ice water
2 tablespoons lemon juice
1½ teaspoons liquid *Sucaryl*

Chill bowl and beater. Mix dry milk and ice water in bowl; beat with electric mixer until soft peaks form. Add lemon juice and *Sucaryl;* beat until stiff peaks form.

Makes 3½ cups, each ¼-cup serving 16 calories; 1.5 grams protein; no fat; 2.5 grams carbohydrate. (With sugar, 32 calories)

1 serving = ¼ cup skim milk

Rum-Flavored Whipped Topping

Prepare Low-Calorie Whipped Topping, adding ¾ teaspoon rum flavoring with the lemon juice and *Sucaryl.*

Makes 3½ cups, each ¼-cup serving 16 calories; 1.5 grams protein; no fat; 2.5 grams carbohydrate. (With sugar, 32 calories)

1 serving = ¼ cup skim milk

Brandy-Flavored Whipped Topping

Prepare Low-Calorie Whipped Topping, adding 1 teaspoon brandy flavoring with the lemon juice and *Sucaryl.*

Makes 3½ cups, each ¼-cup serving 16 calories; 1.5 grams protein; no fat; 2.5 grams carbohydrate. (With sugar, 32 calories)

1 serving = ¼ cup skim milk

Orange-Flavored Whipped Topping

Prepare Low-Calorie Whipped Topping, adding ¾ teaspoon orange flavoring with the lemon juice and *Sucaryl*.

Makes 3½ cups, each ¼-cup serving 16 calories; 1.5 grams protein; no fat; 2.5 grams carbohydrate. (With sugar, 32 calories)

1 serving = ¼ cup skim milk

Cheese Dessert Topping

This orange- and lemon-flavored topping can also double as a smooth, creamy frosting for cakes.

> 1 8-ounce package **Neufchatel cheese**
> 2 tablespoons liquid *Sucaryl*
> **Dash of salt**
> 1 tablespoon **grated lemon rind**
> 1 tablespoon **lemon juice**
> 1 tablespoon **grated orange rind**
> 1 tablespoon **orange juice**

Let cheese soften at room temperature. Combine all ingredients in mixer bowl and blend until smooth and creamy. Chill well. Serve as topping over gingerbread, stewed fruit or pudding.

Makes 1 cup, each tablespoon 36 calories; 1.5 grams protein; 3 grams fat; 0.5 gram carbohydrate. (With sugar, 90 calories)

1 serving = 1 fat exchange

Thick Custard Cream (*Crème Pâtissière*)

3 egg yolks
2 teaspoons liquid *Sucaryl*
½ cup nondairy powdered creamer
¼ cup flour
1 cup boiling water
1½ teaspoons butter
2 teaspoons vanilla
  (or ½ teaspoon vanilla plus
  other flavoring, as desired)

In a heavy-bottomed saucepan, combine egg yolks and
Sucaryl; beat for 2 to 3 minutes until mixture is pale yellow.
Combine powdered creamer and flour; beat into egg yolks.
(Mixture will be very thick.) Gradually beat in boiling water
in a thin stream. Place over moderate heat and beat vigor-
ously with a wire whip. When the boil is reached, immediately
reduce heat to very low, and continue to cook and beat for
2 to 3 minutes, being careful not to scorch custard. Remove
from heat and beat in butter and flavoring. Chill well before
using as a filling.

Makes 1½ cups, each tablespoon 25 calories; 0.5 gram protein;
1.5 grams fat; 2 grams carbohydrate. (With sugar, 37 calories)

4 tablespoons = ½ bread exchange
1 fat exchange

Lemon Custard Cream

Prepare Thick Custard Cream recipe, adding ¼ cup lemon juice and the grated rind of 1 lemon with the boiling water.

Makes 1½ cups, each tablespoon 25 calories; 0.5 gram protein; 1.5 grams fat; 2 grams carbohydrate. (With sugar, 37 calories.)

4 tablespoons = ½ bread exchange
1 fat exchange

Custard Chiffon

Prepare Thick Custard Cream recipe, folding 3 stiffly beaten egg whites into the custard while it is still warm. Chill before using.

Makes 3 cups, each ¼-cup serving 54 calories; 2 grams protein; 3.5 grams fat; 4 grams carbohydrate. (With sugar, 78 calories)

½ cup = ½ bread exchange
1 fat exchange
½ meat exchange

Lemon Custard Chiffon

Prepare Lemon Custard Cream recipe, folding 3 stiffly beaten egg whites into the custard while it is still warm. Chill before using.

Makes 3 cups, each ¼-cup serving 55 calories; 2 grams protein; 3.5 grams fat; 4.5 grams carbohydrate. (With sugar, 78 calories)

½ cup = ½ bread exchange
1 fat exchange
½ meat exchange

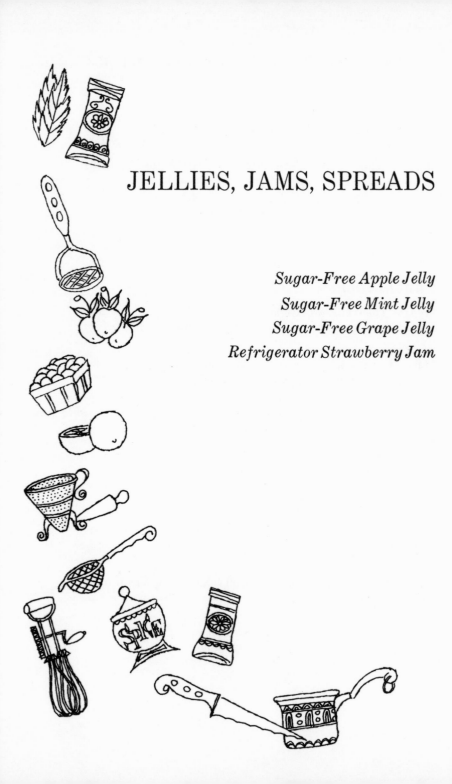

JELLIES, JAMS, SPREADS

Sugar-Free Apple Jelly
Sugar-Free Mint Jelly
Sugar-Free Grape Jelly
Refrigerator Strawberry Jam

Refrigerator Plum Jam
Refrigerator Peach Jam
Refrigerator Grape Jam
Refrigerator Apple Butter

In the following sugar-free jelly recipes a small amount of unflavored gelatin is used to give the jellies a proper spreading consistency. No additional pectin is required. You will note that these low-calorie jellies should be kept in the refrigerator (or in the freezer if large batches are made at one time). The jellies may be made so quickly and easily that you will probably find it preferable to make a small quantity as you need it.

Sugar-Free Apple Jelly

4 teaspoons unflavored gelatin	1½ tablespoons lemon juice
2 cups unsweetened apple juice	Yellow food coloring,
2 tablespoons liquid *Sucaryl*	as desired

Soften gelatin in ½ cup of the apple juice. Bring remaining 1½ cups juice to the boil; remove from heat. Add softened gelatin, stirring to dissolve. Add *Sucaryl*, lemon juice and food coloring, as desired. Bring to the full rolling boil. Ladle into clean half-pint jars; seal. Keep in refrigerator.

Makes 2 half-pint jars, each tablespoon 9 calories; 0.5 gram protein; no fat; 2 grams carbohydrate. (With sugar, 36 calories)

If no more than 1 tablespoon is used, need not be calculated as exchanges. If larger amounts are used; 2 tablespoons = ½ fruit exchange.

Sugar-Free Mint Jelly

Prepare Apple Jelly as directed, adding this extra step: Wash, drain and lightly crush 1½ cups firmly packed mint leaves. Steep in boiling apple juice 10 minutes. Strain and add green food coloring as desired. Proceed as for Apple Jelly.

Nutritional analysis same as for Sugar-Free Apple Jelly.

Sugar-Free Grape Jelly

4 teaspoons unflavored gelatin	1½ cups unsweetened grape juice
½ cup water	2 tablespoons liquid *Sucaryl*

Soften gelatin in water. Bring grape juice to the boil; remove from heat. Add softened gelatin, stirring to dissolve. Add *Sucaryl*. Bring to the full rolling boil. Ladle into clean half-pint jars; seal. Keep in refrigerator.

Makes 2 half-pint jars, each tablespoon 9 calories; 0.5 gram protein; no fat; 2 grams carbohydrate. (With sugar, 36 calories)

If no more than 1 tablespoon is used, need not be calculated as exchanges. If larger amounts are used, 2 tablespoons = ½ fruit exchange.

Sugar-Free Jams (Long-Boil Method)

To make *Sucaryl*-sweetened jams, follow tested recipes for jams made by the long-boil method without the addition of pectin. Cook the fruit with *Sucaryl* (2 tablespoons liquid *Sucaryl* for each cup of sugar ordinarily used) until jam is of desired consistency. Pour the boiling-hot jam into clean hot jars, sealing each jar as soon as it is filled. Long cooking sterilizes the fruit, so that with an airtight seal, spoilage will not occur.

Sugar-Free Jams (Gelatin Method)

In the following refrigerator jams, proper spreading consistency is achieved through the use of a small amount of unflavored gelatin. Since these jams must be refrigerated, make a small amount at a time, as you need it. If you prefer to make a large batch, the jam may be stored in the freezer.

Refrigerator Strawberry Jam

1½ teaspoons unflavored gelatin
1½ tablespoons cold water
3 cups strawberries, crushed
1½ tablespoons liquid *Sucaryl*
¼ teaspoon ascorbic acid powder
Red food coloring, as desired

Soften gelatin in cold water. Combine strawberries and *Sucaryl* in saucepan. Place over high heat and stir constantly until mixture comes to the boil. Remove from heat; add softened gelatin; return to heat and continue to cook for 1 minute. Remove from heat; blend in ascorbic acid powder and food coloring if necessary. Ladle into clean half-pint jars; seal. Store in refrigerator.

Makes 2 half-pint jars, each tablespoon 5 calories; trace of protein; trace of fat; 1 gram carbohydrate. (With sugar, 26 calories)

If no more than 1 tablespoon is used, need not be calculated as exchanges. If larger amounts are used, 4 tablespoons = ½ fruit exchange.

Refrigerator Plum Jam

> 2 teaspoons unflavored gelatin
> 1 tablespoon cold water
> 2½ pounds Damson plums
> ½ cup water
> 4 tablespoons liquid *Sucaryl*

Soften gelatin in cold water. Wash, remove stems, halve and pit the plums. Place in kettle with water. Cook over medium heat, stirring occasionally, until plums are soft; crush lightly. Measure fruit, add water, if necessary, to make 4 cups pulp. Add *Sucaryl* and softened gelatin. Return to heat and continue to cook for 1 minute. Remove from heat; ladle into clean half-pint jars; seal. Store in refrigerator.

Makes 4 half-pints, each tablespoon 9 calories; trace of protein; no fat; 2 grams carbohydrate. (With sugar, 36 calories)

If no more than 1 tablespoon is used, need not be calculated as exchanges. If larger amounts are used, 2 tablespoons = ½ fruit exchange.

Refrigerator Peach Jam

2 teaspoons unflavored gelatin
1 tablespoon cold water
3½ pounds fresh peaches
4 tablespoons liquid *Sucaryl*
8 teaspoons lemon juice

Soften gelatin in cold water. Peel, pit and cut peaches into pieces. Place in kettle without water. Cook over medium heat, stirring occasionally, until peaches are soft; crush lightly. Measure fruit; add water, if necessary, to make 4 cups pulp. Add *Sucaryl*, lemon juice and softened gelatin. Return to heat and continue to cook for 1 minute. Remove from heat; ladle into clean half-pint jars; seal. Store in refrigerator.

Makes 4 half-pints, each tablespoon 10 calories; trace of protein; no fat; 2.5 grams carbohydrate. (With sugar, 37 calories)

If no more than 1 tablespoon is used, need not be calculated as exchanges. If larger amounts are used, 2 tablespoons = ½ fruit exchange.

Refrigerator Grape Jam

2 teaspoons unflavored gelatin
1 tablespoon cold water
3 pounds Concord grapes
⅓ cup water
2 tablespoons liquid *Sucaryl*

Soften gelatin in cold water. Wash grapes and place in kettle with water. Cook over medium heat, stirring constantly, until grapes are soft. Remove from heat; force grapes through food mill to remove seeds and skins. Measure; add water, if necessary, to make 4 cups pulp. Add *Sucaryl* and softened gelatin. Return to heat and continue to cook for 1 minute. Remove from heat; ladle into clean half-pint jars; seal. Store in refrigerator.

Makes 4 half-pints, each tablespoon 12 calories; 0.5 gram protein; trace fat; 2.5 grams carbohydrate. (With sugar, 25 calories)

If no more than 1 tablespoon is used, need not be calculated as exchanges. If larger amounts are used, 2 tablespoons = ½ fruit exchange.

Refrigerator Apple Butter

> 2 pounds tart apples
> 2 cups water
> 3 tablespoons liquid *Sucaryl*
> ¼ teaspoon cinnamon
> ⅛ teaspoon allspice
> ⅛ teaspoon powdered cloves
> 1½ teaspoons unflavored gelatin
> ¼ cup cold water

Pare, core and quarter apples. Combine with water, *Sucaryl* and spices; blend a little at a time in electric blender until mixture is smooth. Turn into saucepan. Cook over low heat, stirring frequently until thickened (about 45 minutes). Soften gelatin in the ¼ cup water; blend into boiling apple butter. Divide among 3 clean half-pint jars; seal. Store in refrigerator.

Makes 2½ cups, each tablespoon 12 calories; trace of protein; no fat; 3 grams carbohydrate. (With sugar, 44 calories)

If no more than 1 tablespoon is used, need not be calculated as exchanges. If larger amounts are used, 2 tablespoons = ½ fruit exchange.

PIES AND TARTS

Low-Calorie Cornflake Crust
Low-Calorie Graham Cracker Crust
Low-Calorie Cottage Cheese Pastry
Fluffy Coconut Pie
Apricot Cloud Pie
Chocolate Chiffon Pie
Eggnog Chiffon Pie
Pumpkin Chiffon Pie
Lemonade Chiffon Pie
Strawberry Chiffon Pie
Pineapple Chiffon Pie
Cointreau Chiffon Pie
Lime Chiffon Pie

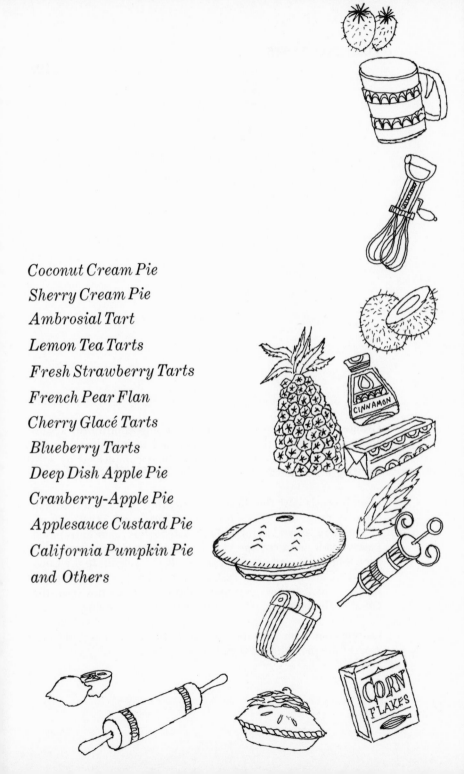

Coconut Cream Pie

Sherry Cream Pie

Ambrosial Tart

Lemon Tea Tarts

Fresh Strawberry Tarts

French Pear Flan

Cherry Glacé Tarts

Blueberry Tarts

Deep Dish Apple Pie

Cranberry-Apple Pie

Applesauce Custard Pie

California Pumpkin Pie

and Others

Granted the pastry surrounding the filling contributes a substantial portion of the calories assigned to any piece of pie, still, worthwhile calorie savings can be accomplished by substituting a noncaloric sweetener for sugar in the fillings.

Crumb crusts cost the dieter considerably fewer calories than a pastry crust. Directions for low-calorie crumb crusts are included here, as well as for a highly satisfactory, calorie-trimmed pastry made with cottage cheese. Normally, a single pie crust for a 9-inch pie contains 657 calories. If you substitute the Low-Calorie Cottage Cheese Pastry for regular pastry in the pie recipes which follow, you may subtract 197 calories from the count of the total pie, or 33 calories from each serving.

Calorie counts for all 9-inch pies have been calculated for one-sixth of the pie, the traditional-sized portion.

Low-Calorie Cornflake Crust

1 cup cornflakes, crushed
2 tablespoons melted butter

1 teaspoon liquid *Sucaryl*

Preheat oven to 350°F. Combine all ingredients. Press firmly into a 9-inch pie plate. Bake 8 to 10 minutes. Chill before filling.

Makes 1 9-inch pie shell, 296 calories; 2 grams protein; 22.5 grams fat; 21.5 grams carbohydrate. (With sugar, 440 calories)

Low-Calorie Graham Cracker Crust

16 small (1 cup) graham
  crackers, crushed

3 tablespoons melted butter
¾ teaspoon liquid *Sucaryl*

Preheat oven to 350°F. Combine all ingredients. Press firmly into a 9-inch pie plate. Bake 8 to 10 minutes. Chill before filling.

Makes 1 9-inch pie shell, 520 calories; 4.5 grams protein; 39.5 grams fat; 42 grams carbohydrate. (With sugar, 628 calories)

Low-Calorie Cottage Cheese Pastry

⅓ cup flour
⅛ teaspoon salt

2 tablespoons shortening
½ cup dry skim-milk cottage cheese

Combine flour and salt; cut in shortening until of consistency of corn meal. Force cheese through sieve; add to flour mixture. Mix with a fork until dough forms a ball. Roll between two sheets of lightly floured waxed paper. (This dough will be softer and more moist than regular pie dough.) Fit into a 9-inch pie plate. Fill with desired filling, and bake as directed for filling used. For a prebaked pie shell, prick shell with a fork and bake 12 to 15 minutes at 450°F.

Makes 1 9-inch pie shell, 460 calories; 25.5 grams protein; 26 grams fat; 30 grams carbohydrate. (Regular pie shell, 657 calories; 10 grams protein; 36.5 grams fat; 71.5 grams carbohydrate.)

Fluffy Coconut Pie

1 envelope unflavored gelatin
½ cup cold water
2 tablespoons liquid *Sucaryl*
3 eggs, separated
½ cup skim milk
1 teaspoon vanilla
¾ cup dried, shredded coconut
1 9-inch baked pie shell

Soften gelatin in cold water. In top of double boiler, combine *Sucaryl*, egg yolks and skim milk. Cook over hot water until mixture thickens. Remove from heat; add vanilla and softened gelatin, stirring to dissolve gelatin. Chill until mixture begins to thicken. Beat egg whites until stiff peaks form; fold into thickened gelatin. Fold in coconut. Spoon into baked pie shell; chill until set. (If desired, garnish top with a little extra coconut.)*

Makes 6 servings, each 204 calories; 7 grams protein; 12 grams fat; 17 grams carbohydrate. (With sugar, 348 calories)

1 serving = 1 bread exchange
1 fat exchange
1 meat exchange

* *For each additional tablespoon of coconut, add 22 calories.*

Pineapple Chiffon Pie

Pineapple was given its name by the English because of its resemblance to the pine cone. Europeans call the fruit *"ananas,"* which is a derivation of the Paraguayan Indian word *"nana,"* meaning "excellent fruit." Use new unsweetened crushed pineapple, as directed here, and you'll call the results an "excellent pie."

> 2 envelopes unflavored gelatin
> 2 cups unsweetened pineapple juice
> 1 1-pound, 4-ounce can unsweetened crushed pineapple
> 2 tablespoons liquid *Sucaryl*
> 4 eggs, separated
> ½ teaspoon salt
> 1 teaspoon grated lemon rind
> 1 tablespoon lemon juice
> 1 9-inch baked pie shell

In top of double boiler, soften gelatin in the pineapple juice. Add crushed pineapple, *Sucaryl*, egg yolks, salt, lemon rind and lemon juice. Cook, stirring occasionally, over hot, not boiling, water, until mixture just begins to thicken (about 20 minutes). Remove from heat; chill until mixture mounds from spoon. Beat egg whites stiff; fold into pineapple gelatin. Spoon into baked pie shell; chill well before serving.

Makes 6 servings, each 268 calories; 9 grams protein; 10 grams fat; 37.5 grams carbohydrate. (With sugar, 412 calories)

> *1 serving = ½ bread exchange*
> *1 fat exchange*
> *3 fruit exchanges*
> *1 meat exchange*

Cointreau Chiffon Pie

1 envelope unflavored gelatin	⅓ cup orange juice
¼ cup cold water	Dash of salt
4 eggs, separated	2 tablespoons Cointreau
4½ teaspoons liquid *Sucaryl*	1 9-inch baked pie shell

Soften gelatin in cold water. Place egg yolks, *Sucaryl*, orange juice and salt in top of double boiler; beat until thick and lemon-colored. Cook over hot water, stirring constantly, until thick and smooth. Remove from heat; add softened gelatin, stirring to dissolve. Blend in Cointreau; chill until mixture begins to thicken. Beat egg whites until stiff peaks form; fold into gelatin mixture. Spoon into baked pie shell; chill until set. Garnish, if desired, with Low-Calorie Whipped Topping, page 178 .

Makes 6 servings, each 186 calories; 7 grams protein; 9.5 grams fat; 14.5 grams carbohydrate. (With sugar, 294 calories)

1 serving = 1 bread exchange
1 fat exchange
1 meat exchange

Apricot Cloud Pie

1½ tablespoons unflavored gelatin	1 1-pint can low-calorie apricot
¼ cup cold water	nectar, heated
1 tablespoon liquid *Sucaryl*	½ cup evaporated milk, chilled
¼ teaspoon salt	1 recipe Low-Calorie Graham
2 tablespoons lemon juice	Cracker Crust, page 193

Soften gelatin in cold water; add *Sucaryl*, salt and lemon juice. Dissolve in hot apricot nectar. Chill until mixture begins to thicken. Beat chilled evaporated milk on high speed of mixer until stiff; fold into gelatin mixture. Pour into baked graham cracker crust. Chill until firm.

Makes 6 servings, each 144 calories; 4.5 grams protein; 8.5 grams fat; 14 grams carbohydrate. (With sugar, 234 calories)

> *1 serving = ½ bread exchange*
> *1 fat exchange*
> *½ fruit exchange*
> *¼ cup milk or ¼ cup skim milk*
> *+ ½ fat exchange*

Chocolate Chiffon Pie

1½ tablespoons unflavored gelatin	2 tablespoons liquid *Sucaryl*
2 cups skim milk	3 eggs, separated
1 ounce unsweetened	1 teaspoon vanilla
chocolate, melted	1 9-inch baked pie shell

In top of double boiler, soften gelatin in ½ cup of the milk; scald remaining milk and add to softened gelatin, stirring to dissolve gelatin. Blend in melted chocolate and *Sucaryl*. Beat egg yolks lightly; add a small amount of the hot liquid to yolks, blending well. Then stir egg-yolk mixture into remaining hot liquid in double boiler; cook over hot water, stirring constantly, until mixture thickens slightly. Remove from heat; blend in vanilla. Refrigerate until mixture begins to mound from spoon. Beat egg whites until soft peaks form; fold into chocolate gelatin. Lightly pile into baked pie shell; chill until set.

Makes 6 servings, each 209 calories; 10 grams protein; 11.5 grams fat; 17.5 grams carbohydrate. (With sugar, 353 calories)

> *1 serving = ½ bread exchange*
> *1 fat exchange*
> *½ meat exchange*
> *½ cup milk or ½ cup skim milk*
> *+ 1 fat exchange*

Eggnog Chiffon Pie

This holiday-minded pie tastes lavishly rich and calorie-laden
... but isn't!

> 1 envelope unflavored gelatin
> ¼ cup cold water
> 1½ cups skim milk
> 1½ tablespoons liquid *Sucaryl*
> ¼ teaspoon salt
> 3 tablespoons cornstarch
> 3 eggs, separated
> 1 teaspoon vanilla
> 1 tablespoon rum flavoring
> 1 9-inch baked pie shell

Soften gelatin in cold water. Combine ¾ cup of the milk, *Sucaryl*
and salt in the top of a double boiler. Stir in paste made from
cornstarch and remaining ¾ cup milk. Cook over boiling water,
stirring constantly until thick. Add a little of the hot mixture
to beaten egg yolks; then stir egg yolk mixture into remaining
hot liquid in double boiler and cook 2 minutes longer. Remove
from heat; stir in softened gelatin until dissolved. Chill until
mixture begins to set. Stir in vanilla and rum flavoring. Fold in
stiffly beaten egg whites. Spoon into baked pie shell. Chill until
firm. Garnish, if desired, with Low-Calorie Whipped Topping,
page 178, and a sprinkling of shaved chocolate.

Makes 6 servings, each 189 calories; 8.5 grams protein; 9 grams
fat; 18.5 grams carbohydrate. (With sugar, 298 calories)

> *1 serving = 1 bread exchange*
> *½ meat exchange*
> *½ cup milk or ½ cup skim milk*
> *+ 1 fat exchange*

Pumpkin Chiffon Pie

It's tantalizingly fragrant with spices, rich-tasting yet delectably light, the perfect ending for a festive holiday dinner.

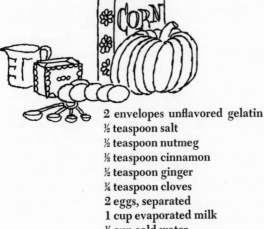

2 envelopes unflavored gelatin
½ teaspoon salt
½ teaspoon nutmeg
½ teaspoon cinnamon
½ teaspoon ginger
¼ teaspoon cloves
2 eggs, separated
1 cup evaporated milk
½ cup cold water
1¼ cups canned pumpkin
4½ teaspoons liquid *Sucaryl*
1 recipe Low-Calorie Cornflake Crust, page 193

Combine gelatin, salt and spices. Beat egg yolks in top of double boiler. Stir in milk, water, pumpkin and *Sucaryl;* then add gelatin-spice mixture. Cook over boiling water until slightly thickened (about 15 minutes). Cool, then refrigerate until thick and syrupy. Beat egg whites until stiff; fold into pumpkin mixture. Spoon into baked cornflake crust and chill until set.

Makes 6 servings, each 160 calories; 8.5 grams protein; 9 grams fat; 11.5 grams carbohydrate. (With sugar, 292 calories)

> 1 serving = ½ bread exchange
> 1 fat exchange
> ½ meat exchange
> 1 "B" vegetable exchange

Lemonade Chiffon Pie

Here's how to drink your lemonade . . . and eat it too! Start with a can of sugar-free frozen lemonade concentrate, and end up with this luscious and low-calorie Lemonade Chiffon Pie.

1½ tablespoons unflavored gelatin	1 tablespoon liquid *Sucaryl*
½ cup cold water	4 eggs, separated
1 tablespoon grated lemon rind	1 5¾-ounce can frozen, low-calorie lemonade concentrate
⅛ teaspoon salt	1 9-inch baked pie shell

Sprinkle gelatin over water in saucepan. Blend in lemon rind, salt, *Sucaryl* and egg yolks. Cook over medium heat, stirring constantly, until slightly thickened and gelatin dissolves. Remove from heat; blend in frozen concentrate, stirring until mixture melts. Refrigerate until mixture begins to thicken. Beat egg whites until stiff peaks form; fold into gelatin. Spoon into baked pie shell; chill until set.

Makes 6 servings, each 176 calories; 8 grams protein; 9.5 grams fat; 13.5 grams carbohydrate. (With sugar, 248 calories)

1 serving = 1 bread exchange
1 fat exchange
1 meat exchange

Lime Chiffon Pie

2 envelopes unflavored gelatin	1½ cups skim milk
½ teaspoon salt	3 eggs, separated
2 teaspoons grated lime rind	Green food coloring
2½ tablespoons liquid *Sucaryl*	1 9-inch baked pie shell
½ cup fresh lime juice	

In top of double boiler, combine gelatin, salt and lime rind. Add *Sucaryl*, lime juice, milk and slightly beaten egg yolks. Cook over hot water until slightly thickened and gelatin is dissolved.

Remove from heat; add food coloring, as desired; chill until mixture begins to mound from spoon. Beat egg whites until soft peaks form; fold into gelatin; chill just until mixture begins to set. Spoon into baked pie shell and chill until set.

Makes 6 servings, each 186 calories; 10 grams protein; 9 grams fat; 17 grams carbohydrate. (With sugar, 366 calories)

> *1 serving = 1 bread exchange*
> *½ meat exchange*
> *½ cup milk or ½ cup skim milk*
> *+ 1 fat exchange*

Strawberry Chiffon Pie

2 envelopes unflavored gelatin	2 eggs, separated
¼ cup cold water	1½ tablespoons liquid *Sucaryl*
1 cup skim milk	2 cups strawberries, crushed
½ cup orange juice	1 9-inch baked pie shell
1 tablespoon grated orange rind	

Soften gelatin in cold water. In top of double boiler, combine milk, orange juice, orange rind, egg yolks and *Sucaryl*. Cook over hot water, stirring constantly, until mixture thickens slightly. Remove from heat; add softened gelatin, stirring to dissolve. Blend in crushed strawberries; chill until mixture begins to set. Beat egg whites until soft peaks form; fold into gelatin. Spoon into baked pie shell and chill until set. If desired, garnish top with Low-Calorie Whipped Topping, page 178, and additional berries.

Makes 6 servings, each 188 calories; 8.5 grams protein; 8 grams fat; 20.5 grams carbohydrate. (With sugar, 296 calories)

> *1 serving = ½ bread exchange*
> *½ fruit exchange*
> *½ meat exchange*
> *½ cup milk or ½ cup skim milk*
> *+ 1 fat exchange*

Coconut Cream Pie

5 tablespoons cornstarch
¼ teaspoon salt
3 cups skim milk, scalded
2 tablespoons liquid *Sucaryl*
3 eggs, well beaten
1 tablespoon butter
1 teaspoon vanilla extract
¼ teaspoon almond extract
½ cup dried, shredded coconut
1 9-inch baked pie shell

In a saucepan, combine cornstarch and salt; gradually blend in scalded milk and *Sucaryl*. Cook over medium heat, stirring constantly, until mixture comes to the boil and thickens; continue to cook 1 minute longer. Gradually add a small amount of the cornstarch mixture to the beaten eggs, blending well. Stir egg mixture into remaining hot liquid in saucepan and continue to cook over low heat, stirring constantly, until mixture is very thick and mounds from spoon. Remove from heat; turn filling into a bowl and stir in the butter, vanilla, almond extract and coconut, mixing well. Cover with plastic or waxed paper and refrigerate 1 hour. Turn into pie shell and refrigerate at least 3 hours before serving.

Makes 6 servings, each 261 calories; 9 grams protein; 13 grams fat; 27 grams carbohydrate. (With sugar, 405 calories)

1 serving = 1½ bread exchanges
1 fat exchange
½ meat exchange
½ cup milk or ½ cup skim milk
+ 1 fat exchange

Coffee Cream Pie

A powdered creamer contributes extra richness of flavor to this excellent pie, and also helps to keep calories under control.

> 1 cup nondairy powdered creamer
> 4 tablespoons cornstarch
> 4 teaspoons instant coffee
> ¼ teaspoon salt
> 2 cups boiling water
> 2 eggs
> 2 tablespoons liquid *Sucaryl*
> 1 tablespoon butter
> 1 teaspoon vanilla
> 1 9-inch baked pie shell

In saucepan, combine powdered creamer, cornstarch, instant coffee and salt. Add boiling water, stirring to blend. Beat eggs and *Sucaryl* together. Add to mixture in saucepan. Cook over medium heat, stirring constantly, until mixture thickens. Remove from heat; blend in butter and vanilla. Chill just until mixture begins to set. Pour into baked pie shell. Refrigerate until set.

Makes 6 servings, each 259 calories; 4.5 grams protein; 16.5 grams fat; 26 grams carbohydrate. (With sugar and light cream, 478 calories)

1 serving = 2 bread exchanges
3 fat exchanges

Sherry Cream Pie

10 tablespoons nondairy powdered creamer
2 envelopes unflavored gelatin
¼ teaspoon salt
3 eggs, separated

4½ teaspoons liquid *Sucaryl*
2½ cups boiling water
6 tablespoons sherry
1 recipe Low-Calorie Graham
Cracker Crust, page 193

In top of double boiler, combine powdered creamer, gelatin, salt, egg yolks and *Sucaryl*. Add boiling water and cook over simmering water, stirring constantly, until mixture is of thin custard consistency. Remove from heat and stir in sherry; chill until mixture begins to mound from spoon. Beat egg whites until soft peaks begin to form; gently fold into gelatin. Spoon into baked graham cracker crust and refrigerate until firm.

Makes 6 servings, each 212 calories; 7 grams protein; 13.5 grams fat; 14 grams carbohydrate. (With sugar and whole milk, 353 calories)

*1 serving = 1 bread exchange
2 fat exchanges
½ meat exchange*

Black-Bottom Pie

Low-calorie version of a featured specialty at Hollywood's Brown Derby.

1 tablespoon cornstarch
2 tablespoons liquid *Sucaryl*
½ teaspoon salt
2 cups skim milk
2 eggs, separated
1 teaspoon vanilla

2 tablespoons cocoa
1 9-inch baked pie shell
1 envelope unflavored gelatin
¼ cup cold water
2 teaspoons rum flavoring

In the top of double boiler, combine cornstarch, 1 tablespoon of the *Sucaryl* and salt. Gradually add milk mixed with egg yolks. Cook over hot water until thick, stirring constantly. Remove from heat; add vanilla. To one cup of the custard mixture, add the remaining 1 tablespoon *Sucaryl* and the cocoa, blending well. Pour into baked pie shell and chill until firm. Soften gelatin in cold water and blend into remaining custard, stirring until dissolved. Stir in rum flavoring. Cool. Beat egg whites stiff and fold into custard. Spoon over chocolate layer and chill until set. If desired, spread top with Low-Calorie Whipped Topping, page 178, and sprinkle with shaved chocolate.

Makes 6 servings, each 181 calories; 8 grams protein; 8.5 grams fat; 18.5 grams carbohydrate. (With sugar, 326 calories)

> *1 serving = ½ bread exchange*
> *½ meat exchange*
> *½ cup milk or ⅓ cup skim milk*
> *+ 1 fat exchange*

Banana "Mock Sour Cream" Pie

Use your blender to make the "mock sour cream" for this luscious banana pie.

1½ cups skim-milk cottage cheese	2 eggs, beaten
1 cup skim milk	1½ tablespoons liquid *Sucaryl*
1 tablespoon lemon juice	1 teaspoon vanilla extract
⅜ teaspoon salt	2 medium bananas
2 tablespoons cornstarch	1 9-inch baked pie shell

Place cottage cheese, milk, 1½ teaspoons of the lemon juice and salt in blender; run a few seconds until smooth. In top of double boiler, combine cornstarch, eggs and *Sucaryl;* blend in cottage-cheese mixture. Cook over boiling water, stirring constantly, until very thick. Remove from heat; add vanilla and chill until mixture just begins to set. Slice bananas and dip pieces in remaining lemon juice to prevent darkening. Place half the banana slices in bottom of baked pie shell; cover with cottage-cheese mixture; then top with remaining banana slices. Chill well before serving.

Makes 6 servings, each 243 calories; 16.5 grams protein; 8 grams fat; 25.5 grams carbohydrate. (With sugar, 351 calories)

> *1 serving = 1 bread exchange*
> *1 fruit exchange*
> *2 meat exchanges*

Ambrosial Tart

2 tablespoons cornstarch	2 eggs, slightly beaten
⅛ teaspoon salt	1 banana, thinly sliced
2 tablespoons liquid *Sucaryl*	¼ cup dried, shredded coconut
1 cup orange juice	1 recipe Low-Calorie Graham
1 8½-ounce can low-calorie	Cracker Crust, page 193
pineapple chunks	

In a saucepan, combine cornstarch, salt, *Sucaryl* and orange juice. Drain pineapple; set fruit aside. Measure liquid and add enough water to make 1 cup. Add to saucepan with the beaten eggs. Cook over medium heat, stirring constantly, until mixture comes to the boil and thickens. Remove from heat and chill well; then fold in the pineapple chunks, sliced banana and coconut. Spoon into baked graham cracker crust and chill until ready to serve.

Makes 6 servings, each 193 calories; 3.5 grams protein; 9.5 grams fat; 25 grams carbohydrate. (With sugar, 355 calories)

1 serving = 1 bread exchange
2 fat exchanges
1 fruit exchange

Chocolate Mint Pie

1½ tablespoons unflavored	2 ounces unsweetened choco-
gelatin	late, cut into pieces
½ cup cold water	½ teaspoon mint extract
3 eggs, separated	¼ cup nonfat dry milk
1¼ cups skim milk	¼ cup ice water
2 tablespoons liquid *Sucaryl*	1 9-inch baked pie shell
¼ teaspoon salt	

Soften gelatin in cold water. In top of double boiler, combine egg yolks, milk, *Sucaryl*, salt and chocolate. Cook over hot water, stirring constantly, until smooth and thickened. Remove from heat; add mint extract and softened gelatin, stirring to dissolve gelatin. Chill until mixture begins to mound from spoon. Beat egg whites stiff; fold into gelatin mixture. Combine nonfat dry milk and ice water, beating on high speed of mixer until soft peaks form; fold into chocolate mixture; chill until mixture begins to set. Spoon into baked pie shell and chill until set.

Makes 6 servings, each 240 calories; 11 grams protein; 14 grams fat; 20 grams carbohydrate. (With sugar 384 calories)

> 1 serving = 1 bread exchange
> 1 fat exchange
> ½ meat exchange
> ½ cup milk or ½ cup skim milk
> + ½ fat exchange

Lemon Tea Tarts

Pastry for a 9-inch shell
2 tablespoons cornstarch
¼ teaspoon salt
1 teaspoon grated lemon rind
3 tablespoons lemon juice

1 cup hot water
1 tablespoon liquid *Sucaryl*
1 egg yolk, beaten
1 teaspoon butter

Preheat oven to 425°F. Roll out pastry and cut into circles to fit 10 small tart pans. Bake 12 minutes, or until golden brown; cool. Combine cornstarch, salt and lemon rind. Blend in lemon juice to make a smooth paste. Gradually add hot water and *Sucaryl*; cook over medium heat, stirring constantly, until thick. Stir a small amount of the hot mixture into beaten egg yolk; then stir egg-yolk mixture into remaining hot liquid in pan and cook 2 minutes longer. Remove from heat; add butter. Cool and spoon into tart shells.

Makes 10 tarts, each 82 calories; 1.5 grams protein; 4.5 grams fat; 9 grams carbohydrate. (With sugar, 125 calories)

> 1 tart = ½ bread exchange
> 1 fat exchange

Fresh Strawberry Tarts

Pastry for a 9-inch shell
1 envelope unflavored gelatin
¼ cup cold water
1 quart small strawberries
3 tablespoons liquid *Sucaryl*
Red food coloring
2 tablespoons lemon juice

Preheat oven to 425°F. Roll out pastry and cut into circles to fit 6 medium tart pans. Bake 12 minutes, or until golden brown; cool.

Soften gelatin in cold water. Wash and cap strawberries; sweeten with *Sucaryl*. Press 1½ cups of the berries through a strainer. Add food coloring, if desired. Add lemon juice and bring to the boil. Remove from heat and add softened gelatin, stirring to dissolve. Chill until mixture begins to thicken. Arrange remaining whole berries in tart shells. Cover with glaze.

Makes 6 servings, each 152 calories; 4 grams protein; 6.5 grams fat; 20.5 grams carbohydrate. (With sugar, 368 calories)

> 1 serving = 1 bread exchange
> 1 fat exchange
> ½ fruit exchange

Fresh Peach Glacé Pie

1 8-ounce jar low-calorie peach preserves
4 cups sliced fresh ripe peaches
1 tablespoon liquid *Sucaryl*
1 9-inch baked pastry shell

Melt peach preserves over low heat; force through sieve. Chill until preserves begin to thicken. Combine peach slices and

Sucaryl, tossing lightly. Arrange fruit in baked shell. Cover with peach glaze. Chill until set.

Makes 6 servings, each 170 calories; 2 grams protein; 6 grams fat; 27.5 grams carbohydrate. (With sugar, 242 calories)

> *1 serving = 1 bread exchange*
> *1 fat exchange*
> *1 fruit exchange*

French Pear Flan

A shallow flan pan with a separate bottom is ideal for this apricot-glazed, sugar-free tart.

> **Pastry for a 9-inch shell**
> ½ cup water
> 2 tablespoons liquid *Sucaryl*
> 1 tablespoon lemon juice
> 8 pears, pared, cored and
>   sliced into sixths
> 1 8-ounce jar low-calorie
>   apricot preserves
> **Nutmeg**

Preheat oven to 425°F. Roll out pastry and fit into a 12-inch tart pan. Bake 12 minutes, or until golden brown; remove from oven and cool. Combine water, *Sucaryl* and lemon juice in a saucepan; add pear slices, a few at a time, and poach about 5 minutes, or until tender. Cool slightly, drain and save ¼ cup of the liquid. Arrange pear slices, spoke fashion, in tart shell. In saucepan, combine apricot preserves and reserved liquid; heat until bubbly. Force through a sieve, then spoon over pear slices to glaze. Sprinkle with nutmeg. Chill until ready to serve.

Makes 8 servings, each 185 calories; 2.5 grams protein; 5 grams fat; 34.5 grams carbohydrate. (With sugar, 293 calories)

> *1 serving = 1 bread exchange*
> *1 fat exchange*
> *2 fruit exchanges*

Cherry Glacé Tarts

Pastry for a 9-inch shell
1 1-pound, 5-ounce can water-
   pack red sour cherries

1 tablespoon cornstarch
1½ tablespoons liquid *Sucaryl*
¼ teaspoon almond extract

Preheat oven to 425°F. Roll out pastry and cut into circles to fit 6 medium tart pans. Bake 12 minutes, or until golden brown; cool. Drain cherries, saving juice. In a small saucepan, blend cherry juice into cornstarch to make a smooth paste. Add *Sucaryl* and cook over medium heat, stirring constantly, until thick and clear. Remove from heat; add almond extract and cool. Place ⅛ cup cherries in each tart shell; cover with glaze; chill before serving.

Makes 6 tarts, each 155 calories; 2.5 grams protein; 6.5 grams fat; 23 grams carbohydrate. (With sugar, 263 calories)

1 serving = 1 bread exchange
1 fat exchange
1 fruit exchange

Blueberry Tarts

Pastry for a 9-inch shell
2 cups blueberries
⅓ cup water

1 tablespoon liquid *Sucaryl*
1½ teaspoons cornstarch

Preheat oven to 425°F. Roll out pastry and cut into circles to fit 6 medium tart pans. Bake 12 minutes, or until golden brown; cool. To make filling, combine blueberries, water and *Sucaryl*. Cook until berries are just tender. Drain, saving juice. Gradually blend the juice into cornstarch in a saucepan. Cook until clear and smooth. Gently combine with berries; cool slightly and spoon into baked tart shells.

Makes 6 tarts, each 140 calories; 2 grams protein; 6.5 grams fat; 19.5 grams carbohydrate. (With sugar, 212 calories)

1 serving = 1 bread exchange
1 fat exchange
½ fruit exchange

Deep Dish Apple Pie

4 teaspoons liquid *Sucaryl*
2 tablespoons flour
⅛ teaspoon salt
½ teaspoon grated lemon rind
2 teaspoons lemon juice

¼ teaspoon nutmeg
½ teaspoon cinnamon
6 cups tart apple slices
Pastry for a 9-inch shell

Preheat oven to 425°F. Combine all ingredients except pastry. Place in a 9-inch deep-dish pie plate. Roll pastry for top crust and place on top of filling. Slash pastry in several places to allow steam to escape during baking. Bake 30 to 45 minutes, or until pastry is golden brown.

Makes 6 servings, each 201 calories; 2.5 grams protein; 6.5 grams fat; 35 grams carbohydrate. (With sugar, 297 calories)

> *1 serving = 1 bread exchange*
> *1 fat exchange*
> *2 fruit exchanges*

Deep-Dish Cherry Pie

2 1-pound, 5-ounce cans
 water - packed red sour cherries
8 teaspoons liquid *Sucaryl*

¼ cup quick-cooking tapioca
Pastry for 1 9-inch pie shell

Preheat oven to 400°F. Drain cherries, saving liquid. Place cherries in a 9-inch deep-dish pie plate. Combine cherry liquid, *Sucaryl* and tapioca, blending well. Let stand 5 minutes. Pour over cherries. Roll out pastry to fit top of pie plate; place over cherries, sealing edge. Slash pastry in several places to allow steam to escape during baking. Bake 60 minutes. Serve warm or chilled.

Makes 6 servings, each 214 calories; 3 grams protein; 6.5 grams fat; 37.5 grams carbohydrate. (With sugar, 406 calories)

> *1 serving = ½ bread exchange*
> *1 fat exchange*
> *3 fruit exchanges*

Green Grape and Apple Pie

3 tablespoons quick-cooking tapicoa
Dash of salt
3 cups pared, cored and sliced apples
2 cups green seedless grapes, halved
1 9-inch unbaked pie shell
½ cup water
2 tablespoons liquid *Sucaryl*
2 tablespoons lemon juice
1 tablespoon melted butter

Preheat oven to 450°F. Combine tapioca and salt; toss with apples and grapes. Turn into unbaked pie shell. Combine water, *Sucaryl*, lemon juice and melted butter; pour over fruit in pie shell. Cover top with a circle of aluminum foil to prevent fruit from drying out during baking. Bake 15 minutes; reduce heat to 350°F. and continue baking for 40 to 45 minutes, or until apples are tender.

Makes 6 servings, each 220 calories; 2.5 grams protein; 8.5 grams fat; 35.5 grams carbohydrate. (With sugar, 364 calories)

> *1 serving = 1 bread exchange*
> *2 fat exchanges*
> *2 fruit exchanges*

Cranberry-Apple Pie

Plump fresh cranberries are just about as American as red, white and blue. The tart-sweet tang of this crimson fruit has added zest to meals since the days of the early Colonists, and even to the Indians before them. The Indians called the cranberry "i-bimi" (sour berry). Because cranberries require a great deal of sweetening to be palatable, calories in cranberry dishes can mount up fast. With the help of calorie-free sweetening, this holiday pie has been de-calorized to but a fraction of its usual count.

2 cups fresh cranberries
1¼ cups water
3 tablespoons liquid *Sucaryl*
2 tablespoons quick-cooking tapioca
1 teaspoon cinnamon
¼ teaspoon salt
1 tablespoon butter
3 cups sliced raw apples
1 9-inch unbaked pie shell

Preheat oven to 425°F. In saucepan, combine cranberries, water, *Sucaryl*, tapioca, cinnamon and salt. Cook over medium heat until mixture thickens and berries begin to pop (about 8 minutes). Blend in butter and apple slices. Pour into unbaked pie shell. Bake 30 minutes, or until apples are done.

Makes 6 servings, each 197 calories; 2 grams protein; 8.5 grams fat; 29.5 grams carbohydrate. (With sugar, 413 calories)

1 serving = 1 bread exchange
2 fat exchanges
1½ fruit exchanges

Rhubarb-Strawberry Casserole Pie

4 cups rhubarb, cut into 1-inch pieces
3 cups strawberries, hulled
1 tablespoon lemon juice
3 tablespoons liquid *Sucaryl*
3 tablespoons quick-cooking tapioca
½ teaspoon nutmeg
Pastry for a 9-inch shell

Preheat oven to 450°F. In a large bowl, combine rhubarb, strawberries, lemon juice and *Sucaryl;* mix lightly. Combine tapioca and nutmeg; toss lightly with fruit. Turn fruit into shallow 1½-quart casserole. Roll out pastry to fit casserole; place over fruit and seal edges. Slash pastry in several places to allow steam to escape during baking. Bake 15 minutes; reduce heat to 350°F. and bake 30 minutes longer, or until crust is golden and fruit is tender.

Makes 6 servings, each 167 calories: 2.5 grams protein; 6.5 grams fat; 25.5 grams carbohydrate. (With sugar, 383 calories)

1 serving = 1 bread exchange
1 fat exchange
1 fruit exchange

Applesauce Custard Pie

1½ cups unsweetened applesauce
½ cup skim milk
2 eggs, beaten
2 tablespoons liquid *Sucaryl*
1 teaspoon lemon juice
1 9-inch unbaked pie shell
Nutmeg

Preheat oven to 425°F. Combine applesauce, milk, beaten eggs,

Sucaryl and lemon juice, blending well. Pour into unbaked pie shell. Bake 60 minutes, or until a knife inserted near center comes out clean. Sprinkle with nutmeg.

Makes 6 servings; each 167 calories; 4.5 grams protein; 8 grams fat; 19.5 grams carbohydrate. (With sugar, 311 calories)

> *1 serving = 1 bread exchange*
> *1 fat exchange*
> *½ fruit exchange*
> *½ meat exchange*

California Pumpkin Pie

> 2 eggs, beaten
> 2 tablespoons liquid *Sucaryl*
> ¾ teaspoon cinnamon
> ¾ teaspoon nutmeg
> ½ teaspoon ginger
> ¼ teaspoon cloves
> 1½ cups canned pumpkin
> ¾ cup evaporated milk
> ¾ cup orange juice
> 1 9-inch unbaked pie shell

Preheat oven to 450°F. Combine eggs, *Sucaryl*, spices and pumpkin, blending well. Add milk and orange juice gradually, stirring until well blended. Pour into unbaked pie shell. Bake 10 minutes; reduce heat to moderate (350°F.) and bake 40 to 50 minutes longer, or until a knife inserted near the center comes out clean.

Makes 6 servings, each 211 calories; 6.5 grams protein; 10.5 grams fat; 23 grams carbohydrate. (With sugar, 355 calories)

> *1 serving = 1 bread exchange*
> *2 fat exchanges*
> *1 "B" vegetable exchange*

SALADS AND

Grapefruit Aspic
Amber Apple Jelly Salad
Ginger Melon Mold
Jellied Ambrosia
Sherry Sunshine Salad
Pineapple-Cheese Salad
Orange Soufflé Salad
Fruit-Studded Ruby Salad
Buttermilk Fruit Salad Mold
Two-Layered Spiced Peach Salad
Cranberry Chiffon Salad
Cranberry Relish Salad
Cucumber Aspic

THEIR DRESSINGS

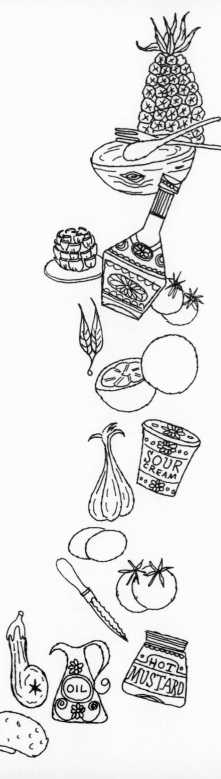

Ever hear: "It's not the potatoes that are fattening, it's the butter or gravy you put on them"? The same is true of salads. Salad greens and many salad fruits and vegetables carry a modest calorie tab . . . it's the dressing that plays havoc with figure-trimming plans.

Fortunately, there are a number of excellent low-calorie dressings on the market, ranging from just 4 to 8 calories per teaspoon. You can also calorie-streamline your own homemade salad dressings so that they may be enjoyed by the most serious of weight watchers.

The secret is to cut down or eliminate the calorie-laden ingredients. Fat, oil and sugar run the calorie count up. On the other hand, lemon juice, vinegar, salt and spices can be used without adding any calories worth counting. Keep fat or oil to a minimum (or omit entirely), and use calorie-free sweetening to replace sugar.

A quivering aspic or jellied salad has special appetite appeal and adds variety and zest to calorie-controlled meals. Low-calorie fruit-flavored gelatins (now available in strawberry, raspberry, orange, cherry, lemon and lime flavors) are a boon to the weight watcher. Plain unflavored gelatin is another ally of the calorie-conscious cook, and can serve as the basis for a myriad of sweet and slimming salads.

Don't forget to use your fancy molds (or go shopping for some new ones if you don't already have an intriguing collection). They'll serve you well, not only for the preparation of the inviting jellied salads that follow, but for the many delightful molded desserts offered under "Desserts, Chilled."

Another weight watcher's trick . . . try serving your salad before the main course, and see how it takes the edge off your appetite.

Grapefruit Aspic

Superb with seafood or chicken, this tart and tantalizing aspic encloses sections of grapefruit and finely chopped celery. Calorie-free sweetening saves you 186 calories in each delightful serving.

> 2 envelopes unflavored gelatin
> ½ cup cold water
> 3 cups unsweetened grapefruit juice
> 3 tablespoons liquid *Sucaryl*
> 3 tablespoons sherry
> 2 cups fresh grapefruit sections
> ¾ cup finely chopped celery

Soften gelatin in cold water. Heat grapefruit juice to boiling; add to gelatin, stirring to dissolve. Add *Sucaryl* and sherry. Arrange a few of the grapefruit sections in the bottom of a lightly oiled 5-cup ring mold to form a decorative pattern; add enough of the gelatin to cover; chill until set. Chill remaining gelatin until it begins to thicken; fold in remaining grapefruit sections and celery. Spoon mixture into mold and chill until firm. To serve, unmold, and if desired, fill center of ring with cottage cheese. Garnish with watercress or other greens.

Makes 7 servings, each 81 calories; 3.5 grams protein; trace of fat; 17 grams carbohydrate. (With sugar, 267 calories)

1 serving = 2 fruit exchanges

Amber Apple Jelly Salad

This is a handsome mold of jellied apple juice, jeweled with grapes, chunks of red-skinned apple and golden pineapple tidbits.

2 envelopes unflavored gelatin
½ cup cold water
1 quart apple juice
1 tablespoon liquid *Sucaryl*
¾ cup diced unpared|apple

¾ cup red or green grape halves, seeded
1 8½-ounce can low-calorie pineapple tidbits, drained

Soften gelatin in cold water. Heat 2 cups of the apple juice; add to gelatin, stirring to dissolve. Add remaining apple juice and *Sucaryl;* chill until mixture begins to thicken. Add diced apple, grapes and pineapple. Spoon into a lightly oiled 6-cup mold; chill until set.

Makes 8 servings, each 106 calories; 2.5 grams protein; trace of fat; 26 grams carbohydrate. (With sugar, 160 calories)

1 serving = 3 fruit exchanges

Ginger Melon Mold

Enjoy this sparkling, icy-cold jellied salad any warm summer day, and feel degrees cooler. It's irresistible . . . and wondrously shy of calories!

2 envelopes unflavored gelatin
½ cup lemon juice
½ cup boiling water

2 tablespoons liquid *Sucaryl*
2 cups noncaloric ginger ale
1½ cups honeydew melon balls

Soften gelatin in lemon juice; add boiling water, stirring to dissolve. Add *Sucaryl* and ginger ale; chill until mixture begins to thicken. Add honeydew melon balls; pour into a lightly oiled 4-cup mold; chill until set. To serve, unmold and garnish with mint, if desired.

Makes 6 servings, each 38 calories; 3.5 grams protein; trace of fat; 6.5 grams carbohydrate. (With sugar, 182 calories)

1 serving = 1 fruit exchange

Jellied Ambrosia

Oranges, bananas and coconut (those made-for-each-other flavors) are embedded in a delectably sweet and fresh-flavored orange jelly.

2 envelopes unflavored gelatin	4½ teaspoons liquid *Sucaryl*
¼ cup cold water	1 cup orange sections
4 cups fresh orange juice	1 cup banana slices
1 tablespoon lemon juice	⅓ cup dried, shredded coconut

Soften gelatin in cold water; dissolve over boiling water. Stir in orange juice, lemon juice and *Sucaryl*; chill until mixture begins to thicken. Fold in fruit and coconut; spoon into a lightly oiled 5-cup mold; chill until set.

Makes 7 servings, each 120 calories; 4 grams protein; 1.5 grams fat; 25.5 grams carbohydrate. (With sugar, 213 calories)

1 serving = 3 fruit exchanges

Sherry Sunshine Salad

3 envelopes unflavored gelatin	½ cup sherry
½ cup cold water	2 tablespoons liquid *Sucaryl*
1½ cups apple juice	½ cup orange sections
2 cups noncaloric ginger ale	1 cup banana slices
1½ cups orange juice	⅓ cup avocado, cubed

In large bowl, soften gelatin in cold water. Bring apple juice to the boil; add to gelatin, stirring to dissolve. Add ginger ale, orange juice, sherry and *Sucaryl*; chill until mixture begins to thicken. Add orange sections, banana slices and cubed avocado. Spoon into a lightly oiled 8-cup mold; chill until set.

Makes 10 servings, each 92 calories; 3 grams protein; 1.5 grams fat; 15 grams carbohydrate. (With sugar, 178 calories)

1 serving = 2 fruit exchanges

Pineapple-Cheese Salad

1 envelope unflavored gelatin	2 tablespoons lemon juice
½ cup cold water	1 tablespoon liquid *Sucaryl*
1½ cups boiling water	1 cup grated sharp cheese
2 8¼-ounce cans low-calorie pineapple tidbits	

Soften gelatin in cold water; add boiling water, stirring to dissolve. Drain pineapple, saving liquid; set fruit aside. Add pineapple liquid, lemon juice and *Sucaryl* to dissolved gelatin. Chill until mixture begins to thicken; fold in pineapple and cheese. Spoon into a lightly oiled 4-cup ring mold; chill until firm. Garnish, if desired, with pineapple slices and cherries.

Makes 6 servings, each 125 calories; 6.5 grams protein; 6 grams fat; 11.5 grams carbohydrate. (With sugar, 197 calories)

1 serving = 1 fruit exchange
1 meat exchange

Orange Soufflé Salad

2 envelopes unflavored gelatin	⅓ cup mayonnaise-type salad dressing
1½ cups orange juice	1 apple, chopped
2 cups boiling water	2 oranges, sectioned
¼ cup lemon juice	
4 teaspoons liquid *Sucaryl*	

Soften gelatin in ¼ cup of the orange juice; add boiling water, stirring to dissolve. Add remaining 1¼ cups orange juice, lemon juice, *Sucaryl* and salad dressing. Beat with rotary beater until well blended. Chill until mixture begins to thicken. Fold in fruit. Pour into a 5-cup mold; chill until set. To serve, unmold and garnish with additional fruit slices and salad greens, as desired.

Makes 7 servings, each 108 calories; 3.5 grams protein; 4.5 grams fat; 16 grams carbohydrate. (With sugar, 191 calories)

1 serving = 1 fat exchange
2 fruit exchanges

Fruit-Studded Ruby Salad

1 envelope low-calorie raspberry gelatin dessert
1¾ cups boiling water
¼ cup lemon juice

1 tablespoon liquid *Sucaryl*
1 cup sliced fresh peaches
1 cup cantaloupe balls

Place gelatin in a bowl. Add boiling water, stirring to dissolve. Add lemon juice and *Sucaryl;* chill until thick and syrupy. Add fruit; spoon into a lightly oiled 4-cup mold. Chill until set.

Makes 6 servings, each 26 calories; 1.5 gram protein; trace of fat; 5 grams carbohydrate. (With sugar, 98 calories)

1 serving = ½ fruit exchange

Buttermilk Fruit Salad Mold

Here's an ideal all-season salad, one that should enjoy many repeat appearances on your table. It might well be the star attraction at a club luncheon, supported by a hot bread or tea sandwiches and a hot beverage.

1 envelope unflavored gelatin
1 8¼-ounce can low-calorie
   fruit cocktail
1 tablespoon liquid *Sucaryl*

1 tablespoon lemon juice
1¼ cups buttermilk
1 teaspoon almond extract

Soften gelatin in liquid drained from fruit cocktail; dissolve over hot water. Add *Sucaryl*, lemon juice, buttermilk and almond extract. Chill until mixture begins to thicken. Fold in drained fruit cocktail. Spoon into a lightly oiled 3-cup mold. Chill until firm. Unmold on salad greens.

Makes 4 servings, each 57 calories; 5 grams protein; trace of fat; 9 grams carbohydrate. (With sugar, 165 calories)

1 serving = ½ fruit exchange
¼ cup skim milk

Two-Layered Spiced Peach Salad

First Layer	Second Layer
1 1-pound can low-calorie sliced peaches	1 envelope unflavored gelatin
¼ cup vinegar	¼ cup lemon juice
1 tablespoon liquid *Sucaryl*	1 tablespoon liquid *Sucaryl*
6 whole cloves	⅓ cup mayonnaise
1 stick cinnamon	½ teaspoon salt
1 envelope unflavored gelatin	½ cup diced celery
¼ cup cold water	

Drain peach slices; measure liquid, adding enough water to make 2 cups. Add vinegar, *Sucaryl*, cloves and cinnamon; simmer 5 minutes. Soften gelatin in cold water. Remove spices from liquid; add liquid to softened gelatin, stirring to dissolve. Dice several peach slices into half of the gelatin mixture. Pour that half into a lightly oiled 5-cup mold; chill until firm. Reserve remaining gelatin mixture.

Soften second envelope of gelatin in lemon juice; dissolve over hot water. Mix dissolved gelatin and *Sucaryl* with the reserved gelatin mixture; chill until mixture begins to thicken. Beat with a rotary beater; then blend in mayonnaise and salt. Fold in celery and remaining peach slices. Pour over chilled first layer in mold. Chill until set. Unmold and garnish, if desired, with salad greens, peach halves and green grapes.

Makes 7 servings, each 75 calories; 3 grams protein; 4 grams fat; 7 grams carbohydrate. (With sugar, 199 calories)

1 serving = 1 fat exchange
1 fruit exchange

Cranberry Chiffon Salad

1 envelope unflavored gelatin	½ cup unsweetened applesauce
1¾ cups cold water	½ cup finely chopped celery
2 cups whole cranberries	¼ cup nonfat dry milk
4½ teaspoons liquid *Sucaryl*	¼ cup ice water

Soften gelatin in ¼ cup cold water. Combine cranberries and remaining 1½ cups water; cook until skins pop and berries are soft. Force through food mill; add softened gelatin, stirring to dissolve. Add *Sucaryl* and applesauce; chill until mixture begins to thicken. Add celery. Combine dry milk and ice water in small bowl of mixer; beat on high speed until of consistency of whipped cream. Fold into cranberry mixture. Spoon into a lightly oiled 4-cup mold. Chill until set.

Makes 6 servings, each 51 calories; 3.5 grams protein; 0.5 gram fat; 9.5 grams carbohydrate. (With sugar, 159 calories)

> 1 serving = ½ fruit exchange
> ¼ cup skim milk

Cranberry Relish Salad

Richly red and packed full of crunchy goodness, this diet-minded salad teams up handsomely with sliced turkey and ham for an eye-catching holiday buffet tray.

2 envelopes unflavored gelatin	2 cups noncaloric ginger ale
1½ cups cold water	1½ cups diced apples
2 cups cranberries	1½ cups diced celery
3 tablespoons liquid *Sucaryl*	

Soften gelatin in ½ cup of the cold water. Combine cranberries and remaining 1 cup water; cook until skins pop. Force through a sieve; add *Sucaryl*. Add sieved cranberries to gelatin, stirring to dissolve. Cool slightly; stir in ginger ale. Refrigerate until mixture begins to thicken. Fold in apples and celery. Pour into a lightly oiled 4-cup mold; chill until set.

Makes 6 servings, each 54 calories; 3.5 grams protein; 0.5 gram fat; 10.5 grams carbohydrate. (With sugar, 270 calories)

> 1 serving = 1½ fruit exchanges

Cucumber Aspic

3 envelopes unflavored gelatin	2 tablespoons vinegar
1½ cups water	½ teaspoon salt
4 teaspoons liquid *Sucaryl*	Green food coloring
2 cups unsweetened pineapple juice	3 medium cucumbers, finely chopped
½ cup lime juice	

Soften gelatin in ½ cup of the water. Bring remaining water to the boil; add to softened gelatin, stirring to dissolve. Blend in *Sucaryl,* pineapple juice, lime juice, vinegar, salt and food coloring as desired. Chill until mixture begins to thicken. Fold in chopped cucumbers. Spoon into a lightly oiled 6-cup mold; chill until set.

Makes 8 servings, each 56 calories; 4 grams protein; trace of fat; 11.5 grams carbohydrate. (With sugar, 128 calories)

1 serving = 1½ fruit exchanges

Golden Glow Salad

2 envelopes unflavored gelatin	2 tablespoons liquid *Sucaryl*
2 1-pound cans low-calorie grapefruit sections	4 teaspoons vinegar
2 cups boiling water	½ teaspoon salt
½ cup lemon juice	2 cups grated carrots

Soften gelatin in liquid drained from grapefruit; add boiling water, stirring to dissolve gelatin. Add lemon juice, *Sucaryl,* vinegar and salt; chill until mixture begins to thicken. Fold in grapefruit sections and grated carrots. Spoon into a lightly oiled 8-cup mold. Chill until firm.

Makes 12 servings, each 43 calories; 2 grams protein; trace of fat; 8.5 grams carbohydrate. (With sugar, 115 calories)

1 serving = 1 fruit exchange

Gardener's Jellied Salad

2 envelopes unflavored gelatin	1 teaspoon salt
½ cup cold water	Yellow food coloring
3 cups boiling water	½ medium cucumber, diced
½ cup lemon juice	12 radishes, sliced
4 teaspoons liquid *Sucaryl*	6 scallions, sliced
1 tablespoon vinegar	

Soften gelatin in cold water; add boiling water, stirring to dissolve. Blend in lemon juice, *Sucaryl*, vinegar, salt and food coloring as desired. Chill until mixture begins to thicken; fold in vegetables. Spoon into a lightly oiled 6-cup mold; chill until set.

Makes 8 servings, each 18 calories; 2.5 grams protein; no fat; 2.5 grams carbohydrate. (With sugar, 90 calories)

1 serving = 1 "A" vegetable exchange

Coleslaw Parfait Salad

2 envelopes unflavored gelatin	¼ teaspoon salt
½ cup cold water	⅓ cup mayonnaise
1½ cups boiling water	1½ cups shredded cabbage
⅓ cup lemon juice	½ cup diced celery
2 tablespoons vinegar	¼ cup chopped green pepper
4 teaspoons liquid *Sucaryl*	2 tablespoons minced onion

Soften gelatin in cold water; add boiling water, stirring to dissolve. Add lemon juice, vinegar, *Sucaryl* and salt; chill until slightly thickened. Fold in remaining ingredients. Pour into lightly oiled 4-cup mold; chill until set. Unmold on salad greens to serve.

Makes 6 servings, each 74 calories; 3.5 grams protein; 5 grams fat; 5 grams carbohydrate. (With sugar, 170 calories)

1 serving = 1 fat exchange
1 "A" vegetable exchange

Three-Bean Salad

1 cup cooked (or canned) green beans
1 cup cooked (or canned) yellow wax beans
1 cup cooked (or canned) red kidney beans
1 medium onion, thinly sliced
¼ cup chopped green pepper
¼ cup chopped celery
2 tablespoons chopped parsley

Low-Calorie Marinade

1 tablespoon liquid *Sucaryl*
1 teaspoon salt
1 teaspoon dry mustard
1 teaspoon pepper
2 tablespoons salad oil
⅔ cup white vinegar

Combine drained vegetables. Combine all ingredients for marinade. Pour marinade over vegetables and refrigerate overnight.

Makes 6 servings, each 103 calories; 3.5 grams protein; 5 grams fat; 13 grams carbohydrate. (With sugar, 175 calories)

1 serving = ½ bread exchange
1 fat exchange
1 "A" vegetable exchange

Garden Relish Salad

4 cups finely chopped green cabbage
¾ cup finely chopped carrot
1 medium green pepper, finely chopped
½ cup finely chopped onion

¾ cup cider vinegar
4½ teaspoons liquid *Sucaryl*
1 tablespoon salt
½ teaspoon mustard seed
½ teaspoon celery seed

In large bowl, combine chopped vegetables. Combine remaining ingredients in a jar and shake well. Pour dressing over vegetables and toss to coat well. Refrigerate, covered, several hours before serving.

Makes 6 cups, each half-cup serving 16 calories; 0.5 gram protein; no fat; 4 grams carbohydrate. (With sugar, 70 calories)

1 serving = ½ "B" vegetable exchange

Celery Seed French Dressing

1 tablespoon liquid *Sucaryl*   1 tablespoon onion flakes
½ cup vinegar   ¾ cup water
⅛ teaspoon salt   ¼ cup salad oil
⅛ teaspoon dry mustard   2 tablespoons celery seed
2 teaspoons paprika

Combine *Sucaryl*, vinegar, salt, mustard, paprika and onion
flakes; bring to the boil and heat 5 minutes. Remove from heat
and add remaining ingredients. Chill before serving. Excellent
with fruit salads or green salads.

Makes 1½ cups, each tablespoon 21 calories; no protein; 2.5
grams fat; trace of carbohydrate. (With sugar, 39 calories)

1 tablespoon = ½ fat exchange

Creamy Fruit Salad Dressing

1½ teaspoons cornstarch   ¼ cup lemon juice
2 egg yolks, well beaten   2 tablespoons liquid *Sucaryl*
½ cup unsweetened pineapple   1½ teaspoons butter
   juice   ¼ cup nonfat dry milk
½ cup orange juice   ¼ cup ice water

In top of double boiler, combine cornstarch, egg yolks, pineapple, orange and lemon juices and *Sucaryl*. Cook over hot
water, stirring occasionally, 15 to 20 minutes, or until thick and
smooth. Remove from heat; blend in butter. Transfer to bowl
and refrigerate until well chilled. Combine nonfat dry milk and
ice water; beat on high speed of mixer until soft peaks begin to
form. Fold into fruit juice mixture. If refrigerated, mix lightly
before serving.

Makes 2 cups, each tablespoon 13 calories; 0.5 gram protein;
0.5 gram fat; 1.5 grams carbohydrate. (With sugar, 40 calories)

¼ cup serving = ½ fruit exchange
½ meat exchange

*If no more than 1 tablespoon is used, need not be calculated as
exchanges.*

Tomato Soup Dressing

1 10½-ounce can condensed
  tomato soup
¼ cup salad oil
¼ cup vinegar
2 teaspoons liquid *Sucaryl*
2 tablespoons chopped onion
½ teaspoon garlic salt

Combine all ingredients and blend well. Chill before serving over vegetable or tossed salads.

Makes 1¾ cups, each tablespoon 26 calories; trace protein; 2 grams fat; 1.5 grams carbohydrate. (With sugar, 36 calories)

1 tablespoon = ½ fat exchange

Citrus Dressing

¼ cup lemon juice
¼ cup unsweetened grapefruit juice
1½ teaspoons liquid *Sucaryl*
1 teaspoon dry mustard
½ teaspoon salt
⅛ teaspoon pepper

Combine all ingredients; blend well. Chill before serving over fruits or salad greens.

Makes a half-cup, each tablespoon 4 calories; no protein; no fat; 1.5 grams carbohydrate. (With sugar, 31 calories)

Need not be calculated as exchanges.

Pineapple-Orange Dressing

4½ teaspoons liquid *Sucaryl*
1 teaspoon dry mustard
1 teaspoon salt
½ cup orange juice
½ cup unsweetened pineapple juice
⅓ cup lemon juice
¼ cup salad oil
1 teaspoon poppy seeds, if desired

In medium bowl of mixer, combine *Sucaryl*, mustard, salt, orange juice, pineapple juice and lemon juice. At medium speed of mixer, gradually add oil until dressing is thick and smooth. Stir in poppy seeds, if desired. Store, covered, in the refrigerator. Shake before using. Serve over fruit salads.

Makes 1½ cups, each tablespoon 26 calories; no protein; 2.5 grams fat; 1.5 grams carbohydrate. (With sugar, 53 calories)

1 serving = ½ fat exchange

Mock Sour Cream Dressing

> 8 ounces skim-milk cottage cheese
> ⅓ cup skim milk
> 1 teaspoon lemon juice
> ¼ teaspoon salt

Combine all ingredients in blender, buzz until smooth and creamy. Refrigerate before serving. Delicious on molded fruit salads or fresh fruit, or as a low-calorie sandwich spread. If a sweet dressing is desired, add *Sucaryl* to taste.

Makes 1 cup, each tablespoon 15 calories; 3 grams protein; no fat; 0.5 gram carbohydrate.

3 tablespoons = 1 meat exchange

Cooked Salad Dressing ⚹1

This creamy-textured lemon-colored dressing is deliciously sweet and tangy—perfect for fruits.

> 3 egg yolks, well beaten
> 1 tablespoon liquid *Sucaryl*
> ½ cup lemon juice
> 2 teaspoons butter
> ⅛ teaspoon salt
> 2 tablespoons skim milk

Combine all ingredients in small saucepan. Cook over medium heat, stirring constantly, until mixture comes to the boil and thickens slightly. Chill. Serve over fruit salads or aspics.

Makes 1 cup, each tablespoon 18 calories; 0.5 gram protein; 1.5 grams fat; 1 gram carbohydrate. (With sugar, 45 calories)

1 tablespoon = ½ fat exchange

Cooked Salad Dressing #2

Note that this mustard-flavored dressing is made with vinegar rather than lemon (as in Cooked Salad Dressing #1). We like it immensely with a cucumber or tomato aspic, with sliced tomatoes, and as a dressing for coleslaw.

> 2 eggs, beaten
> 4 teaspoons liquid *Sucaryl*
> ⅔ cup skim milk
> ½ cup vinegar
> 1 teaspoon prepared mustard
> ½ teaspoon salt
> ⅛ teaspoon pepper
> ½ teaspoon butter

Combine all ingredients in top of double boiler. Cook over hot, not boiling, water; stir until thick and smooth. Chill. Use to dress coleslaw, aspic salad or tomatoes.

Makes 1½ cups, each tablespoon 10 calories; 0.5 gram protein; 0.5 gram fat; 0.5 gram carbohydrate. (With sugar, 34 calories)

If no more than 1 tablespoon is used, need not be calculated as exchanges.

Sucaryl-Sugar Equivalencies

Sucaryl Liquid	Sucaryl Tablets	Sucaryl Granulated Concentrate	Sucaryl Liquid Concentrate	Sugar
⅛ teaspoon	1	2 shakes	2 drops	1 teaspoon
⅜ teaspoon	3	6 shakes	6 drops	1 tablespoon
1 teaspoon	8	½ teaspoon	16 drops	8 teaspoons
1½ teaspoons	12	¾ teaspoon	24 drops (⅛ teaspoon)	¼ cup
2 teaspoons	16	1 teaspoon	32 drops	⅓ cup
1 tablespoon	24	1½ teaspoons (1 measuring cap)	¼ teaspoon	½ cup
2 tablespoons	48	1 tablespoon (2 measuring caps)	½ teaspoon	1 cup

INDEX

About the Author

SARA HERVEY WATTS, whose articles on food appear regularly in magazines and newspapers throughout the country, is a recognized authority in the field of food. Before becoming home economics consultant to Abbott Laboratories, Mrs. Watts was foods editor of a national consumer magazine. She has also been foods consultant to major manufacturers, advertising agencies and trade associations.

Mrs. Watts lives in Radnor, Pennsylvania, in her 1797 home "Redloft," which also serves as her workshop and the background for many of the handsome food photographs which she plans and supervises.